ROUGH DIAMONDS

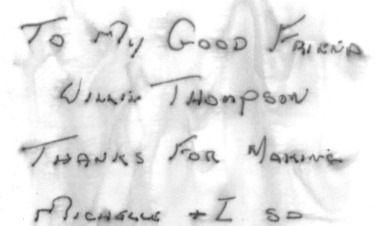

To My Good Friend
Willie Thompson
Thanks For Making
Michaela + I so
Welcome at
Spartan Boxing Club

Bill...

ROUGH DIAMONDS

NOEL DAVIDSON

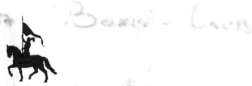

AMBASSADOR INTERNATIONAL
Greenville, South Carolina • Belfast, Northern Ireland

ROUGH DIAMONDS
© Copyright 2006 Noel Davidson

ISBN 1 84030 175 9

Ambassador Publications
a division of
Ambassador Productions Ltd.
Providence House
Ardenlee Street,
Belfast,
BT6 8QJ
Northern Ireland
www.ambassador-productions.com

Emerald House
427 Wade Hampton Blvd.
Greenville
SC 29609, USA
www.emeraldhouse.com

CONTENTS

Part Two: The Paul Winter Story

INTRODUCTION

THE STORY OF how this book came about dates back to before the publication of my last one.

It began when I was planning a launch night for 'As White As Snow,' in Emmanuel, Lurgan, and recounting some of the gripping incidents from the book to Philip and Jill Emerson. They listened with interest and at one point Philip remarked quite casually, "We have a character like that here. You ought to consider writing about Paul Winter sometime."

Same thing happened in Ahoghill. I was discussing details of the launch night programme in The Wash Basin with Sharon Hutchinson, my contact and a capable event convenor, when she asked, "Did you ever hear of Billy Morgan, a great wee guy who works here? He has an amazing testimony, too."

I met both these men in the separate venues in November last year. Paul Winter came across to the table where Debbie Forrest and I were signing copies of her story. After having his book signed he introduced himself and said, "People have told me that I ought to write my story but I wouldn't have a notion about how to do that. Would you have time to do it for me?" It was difficult to hear all the high points of his colourful life with so many people around but I gleaned enough from what he said to whet my appetite. I promised him I would consider it, and took a note of his phone number.

One of the first people we met next night when we arrived in the Wash Basin was a squat, tough-looking little man, no hair and all smiles. His neck and head seemed fused into one stiff block but he appeared to have the muscular body of a weightlifter. Snippets of information that I picked up when I heard him chatting to Debbie, Ali and Brenda, all former drug-addicts now serving the Lord, and my wife, Liz, made me think, 'Sharon was right. This is another fantastic Christian character.'

It was Billy Morgan.

When I came to consider the matter I realised that if these two men's life stories were to go into the same book they would make not only fascinating but also challenging reading.

Thus it was that in the early part of 2006 that I embarked on this project, and in doing so, I was, as the work progressed, struck by two things. The most obvious of these was how loving, longsuffering and merciful our God is, having preserved the lives of these two lawless individuals and then having saved each of them in such a miraculous way. The other noticeable fact that was to unfold was how similar their lives were. They had both come from a profligate background through to a life-changing encounter with God and then on into Christian outreach on the streets where they had once been renowned for their love of liquor rather than, as now, their love of the Lord.

There were significant differences too, but I won't outline them. That is left to the reader to compare the two stories and make up his or her own mind what they are.

It has been a pleasure to research this book with Billy and Paul. Their enthusiasm for having their stories put into print has been most encouraging. They would be the first to stress however, that this is not to bring any gain or glory to them, for their early lives were, as you will discover while you read, anything but glorious! It is that others may be contacted for Christ.

No matter what job we undertake in Christian service we invariably find ourselves relying on the help and support of others of like mind. This has been the case for me during this project and in that context I would like to thank Veronica in Emmanuel, and Sharon and the staff of the Upper Room Restaurant in the Wash Basin, for all the friendship, cooperation and support shown to me over the past seven or eight months.

Catchy titles are sometimes hard enough to come up with but this one came out of a remark by a speaker during a church service. Referring to someone who had once been a wild man in his hometown he described him as ' a rough diamond right enough.'

I thought, 'That's it! Thank you, Joe. That's them! Billy and Paul! Rough as they come but now shining like diamonds for Jesus!'

On behalf of all those involved in the production of this book, and particularly the publisher and Paul and Billy, the 'Rough Diamonds,' themselves, I commend it to you.

We hope that you will find it both an interesting and inspirational read, but more than that. It is our desire and prayer that through reading these two stories you will have a memorable experience with God. If you are a Christian we trust that they may cause you to rejoice in the wonder of salvation. If you haven't come to Jesus we pray that you may do so, and allow Him to transform you into the precious gem He wants you to be in His kingdom.

Noel Davidson
September 2006.

PART ONE

The
Billy Morgan
Story

1

DEATH BEFORE DISHONOUR

THERE WAS AN uncanny silence in the car.

The two Billys were barely speaking to each other, and that was unusual.

Twenty-one year old Billy Morgan from Ballymena had been in the Royal Navy, serving with the Royal Marine Commandos for two years. He had been home on leave in Northern Ireland for a fortnight and was returning to his unit in Portsmouth.

His cousin Billy Kenny, who had also come from the County Antrim town, was serving with the Ulster Defence Regiment and was stationed in Belfast. He had picked Billy Morgan up from the train at York Street station in the city and was giving him a lift on the short journey across to the docks to catch the Heysham ferry.

The two young men had always been close friends and usually had a lively chat when Billy K was available to taxi Billy M from train to boat. They had similar interests and were both serving in 'the forces' and so there was generally a high-spirited exchange between them when they met.

It was totally different this particular evening, though.

There were no jokes, no laughs, no yarns. Indeed there was little or no communication.

There could be either one of two reasons for this weird wordlessness. Or perhaps it stemmed from a combination of both.

It was mid-March 1973 and 'The Troubles' were at their worst. Tensions were running high in Belfast and with Billy Kenny's UDR connection perhaps he was feeling under threat.

What stunned Leading Seaman Morgan into not being able to think of even a sensible sentence to say, though, was the presence of the woman in the car.

When his cousin picked him up from the station he had put his bag in the boot and opened a back door for him. That was when he first sensed that 'something funny' was going on. They usually sat side by side in the front, just the two of them. The returning seaman duly clambered into the back seat, as he was obviously supposed to do, only to discover that there was a woman sitting in the front passenger seat.

This startled Billy. He knew that his cousin was a married man with two young children. Who was this woman sitting beside him, staring fixedly ahead in sullen silence? Was Billy having an affair, or was there something even more sinister to it than that?

Billy felt totally uneasy. There was something awfully wrong here, but he couldn't pinpoint what it was. It was creepy.

When they arrived at the ferry terminal Billy Kenny came round to the back of the car as Billy Morgan was about to retrieve his bag and walk away. The driver took the bag, probably as an excuse to accompany his passenger into the building, from which he would board the steamer.

They had just entered the terminal when Billy Kenny said, hastily, "Billy, I want you to promise me something."

"What's that?" his cousin replied, having a fair idea what was coming.

"Promise me that you won't tell anybody about that girl in the car," he urged.

"Of course I won't, Billy. Don't worry," came the assurance. It was flippant, it was delivered with a quick, knowing laugh, but it was his promise, nonetheless.

They parted with that, Billy Kenny back towards the car with the strange woman in it, Billy Morgan to join the queue for the boat.

As he looked for somewhere to stretch out for a sleep on the overnight sailing Billy chuckled inwardly. 'Good old Billy,' he thought. 'He always was a bit of a flyboy. He's certainly having a good time to himself.'

An instant shadow then crossed his mind at that point. It had struck him that Billy didn't actually look like somebody who was 'having a good time to himself.' Perhaps, though, it was just the pangs of conscience that were pricking him, having been in the company of 'another woman.' Anyway, Billy knew his own business best. He would need to get an hour or two's sleep...

When he arrived back in Portsmouth to report to his unit in the early afternoon Billy was surprised to find two military policemen waiting for him at the dockyard gate. They asked him a few questions and when Billy had confirmed his identity they ordered him to come with them.

As they escorted him through the naval dockyard Billy's heart was racing. 'What have I done?' he wondered. 'I have just been on leave so I couldn't have been involved in anything here.'

He hadn't long to wait for an explanation, however.

His escorts brought him to the office of the Commanding Officer and when Billy saw this the colour drained from his face and he felt sick with fear.

The two policemen showed him in and the CO invited Billy to take a seat in front of him. Recognising the gravity of the message he had to deliver, the Commanding Officer wasted no time in coming to the point.

"Do you know Corporal William Kenny of the Ulster Defence Regiment?" he enquired at once.

"Corporal William Kenny," Billy repeated, to give himself some thinking and composure time. He wasn't used to hearing his cousin referred to as 'William,' but he knew who the CO meant.

"Yes," he went on. "Corporal William Kenny. I know him. He is my cousin. I know him as Billy. Would that be him?"

"Yes, that's him," the Commanding Officer confirmed, slowly. He allowed himself a short pause and a long intake of breath before continuing, "I have some bad news for you. Corporal Kenny was kidnapped and murdered last night. His body was found dumped on waste ground somewhere in Belfast. He had been shot in the head."

Billy sat speechless, motionless and numb.

The Commanding Officer allowed him to come to terms with the shocking fact of his cousin's death, before informing him, "We understand that you were with him last night. As you were one of the last people to see him alive, detectives will be coming over from Northern Ireland to question you tomorrow about what you remember. They think you might have information that could help them."

What a dilemma. One of his best mates had been murdered, and he was a vital witness, who could possibly provide information that would put the authorities on the track of his killers.

Yet on the other hand he had made a promise to his cousin that he wouldn't tell anybody about the woman in the car. Could she be in some way connected with Billy's kidnap and murder? He had no way of knowing. Maybe she had, maybe she hadn't. If he disclosed about her, though, so many family members would be hurt.

Could he break his promise?

When the team came over to interview him Billy answered their questions about times as precisely as possible, but his conscience told him that he was being less than honest when he described Billy as 'appearing like his normal self.'

There were moments during the questioning that he was on the verge of coming out with all he knew and yet something held him back. It was possibly a strange sense of loyalty to his now-dead friend that prevented him from telling all he knew. Rightly or wrongly, Billy didn't divulge the full story.

Before they left to return to the trouble-torn province, the interviewing officers told Billy that they would be recommending to his Commanding Officer that he should 'not be granted leave to go back to Northern Ireland in the foreseeable future.' They considered that his life could be in danger as he had been with Corporal Kenny on that fatal night. And they didn't know the half of it!

It was just a week later that Billy sailed for Malta with his secret intact.

He was glad to be sailing south, the farther from Northern Ireland the better. Perhaps the constant call to duty would bring some relief to his grieving heart and troubled conscience.

It didn't though.

Still it niggled him.

Had he done the right thing?

Four months later, after his tour of duty was over, Billy had a period of leave. As he wasn't permitted to go back to Ballymena he decided to meet up with another cousin who lived in England and go to Nuneaton for the weekend.

Billy's cousin had a special reason for wanting to go to Nuneaton. He had heard of a particularly good tattoo artist who lived there and he wanted to have a tattoo done.

This gave Billy an idea. Why should he not have one as well?

As the needles burnt into his right forearm and the words below the elaborate tattoo began to appear, he experienced a certain sense of vindication.

When it was finished Billy turned his arm around so that he could read the three words burnt into it forever.

They conveyed a message that was both striking and strong in its stark simplicity.

It was DEATH BEFORE DISHONOUR

2

COULD YOU LIVE WITH THE SHAME?

BILLY'S TERM IN the navy ended in December 1974 and he returned to Northern Ireland where he enlisted in the Ulster Defence Regiment early in 1975. He felt that by doing so he was helping to defend his country, but that was not the only reason. There was also a sense in which he felt that he owed it to the memory of his cousin Corporal Kenny, to carry on the family tradition, which had been so tragically terminated for him. Billy was stationed in the Ballymena depot and had served for almost a year with the regiment when events in his life were to take another terrible turn.

It was Christmas Eve and he was out celebrating with a few of his friends. Private Morgan had been on duty all the night before and also for a greater part of the day. He was tired, but relieved to be off for a short time over the holiday period, and was determined to live it up.

As the evening progressed Billy and his companions pitched from one pub to another, meeting mates and consuming substantial quantities of alcohol. It was 'the season to be merry,' they had been led to believe, and 'merry' was what they were bent on being.

About midnight a scuffle broke out in the Ballymena bar where they were drinking at that particular time. A stupid comment was passed by one of the revellers, who had become increasingly loud in what they said and increasingly irresponsible for what they did. Billy took personal exception to the remark and challenged the man who had made it, very aggressively.

The war of words quickly deteriorated into a flailing of fists, and Billy, having been seen as the prime agitator, was forcibly evicted from the bar.

He was angry.

He was under the influence of alcohol.

He was in no fit state to drive a car.

That didn't stop him trying it, though.

One of his companions, who had been trying to pull him away from the fracas, accompanied him out of the bar. Both of them stood for a while shouting abuse at the door, which was now firmly closed against them. It eventually dawned on them that this was a lost cause, and so they gave up.

When they had lurched up to Billy's car he said to his friend, "Climb in there and I will give you a lift home."

The mate did as he was instructed and somehow Billy was able to find his house and leave him off. Just before he closed the door to walk unsteadily away the friend called "Merry Christmas, Billy," into the car.

"Merry Christmas!" the man behind the wheel replied in a groggy irony. Billy's befuddled mind was slowly becoming engulfed in a sullen stroppy stupor.

Then with loud revs cutting into the quiet of the first hour of Christmas Day he shot off into the night...

When he returned to the real world Billy felt something

warm running down his face. It was blood, his own sticky blood. His instant reaction was to try and lift a hand to wipe it away, but he was immediately to discover that he couldn't.

There was something wrong with his eyes. He tried to peer around with whatever vision he could muster and all he could see ahead was a tangle of mangled metal. There was no windscreen in front of him any more, just this mass of metal. And it was red metal.

This seemed to stir him into some kind of sensible reasoning. 'Red metal,' he thought, trying hard to focus his beleaguered mind. 'Red metal... But my car is blue...'

Unable to solve this mystery he slumped forward and looked down as he did so. This brought another surprise. One of his legs, he couldn't make out which, had something white sticking out of it. Could it be a bone?

Still struggling to come to terms with what had actually happened to him, Billy was surprised that he didn't feel any pain. His body was obviously badly smashed up but why was he not in pain? He couldn't understand it.

Having sat there stunned, trapped in a crushed car for some time, Billy gradually became aware that there were people around. He could hear noises and voices, and one of the voices was speaking to him.

"Don't worry," the paramedic was saying, "we are going to give you something to allow the firemen to get you out."

It was four o'clock on Christmas afternoon when Billy Morgan regained consciousness. As he came back to his senses, he thought that he must be in hospital. He was certainly in a bed, somewhere, and there were Christmas decorations above his head and what looked like Christmas cards pinned to a wall opposite.

Realising that he couldn't see very clearly Billy put his hand up, only to discover that his right eye was heavily bandaged.

"I've lost my eye," was his immediate panic-stricken reaction. His leg was also strapped up and he was stiff and sore all over.

Having recovered sufficiently to recognise that he was in hospital Billy became aware that there were two people sitting in silent vigil beside his bed. Raising his head ever so slightly he saw that it was his father and mother.

They both appeared extremely worried. Or was it upset? Or angry? Or embarrassed? Was it just that they were gravely worried about him, or was there something else?

His parents weren't saying much, just sitting with that deep and distant, shocked and stunned look about them. Why were they not leaning over his bed, telling him how sorry they were that this, whatever it was, had happened to him?

"Where am I?" Billy asked, at length. "What is going on?"

"You are in the Waveney Hospital," his father was first to inform him. "You have been in an accident, and that's why you are here."

"An accident," Billy echoed the words. "Where? When?"

He lay back on the pillow and slowly it came back to him. The thing sticking out of his leg. The red paint. No windscreen. The smell of petrol. Flashing lights. Uniforms. The sound of voices...

His parents were in no hurry to fill him in on the details. They just didn't know where to start, for they weren't even sure how they felt, or how to say what they had to tell him.

It was his father who again eventually found the words to explain the events of the night before. "It was about one o'clock this morning, out on the Cushendall Road, only a quarter of a mile or so from here that it happened," he began. "As far as we can make out you were drunk and smashed into a car coming the other way."

Billy was by now alert enough to appreciate that there could be terrible consequences resulting from what he had just been told. "And the people in the other car. What about them?" he enquired eagerly, earnestly and anxiously. A sudden inexplicable sense of foreboding had descended upon him. "Are they O.K.?"

There was another long pause, and then it was mother's turn.

"No, Billy, they are not O.K." she told him, making no attempt to wipe away the tears that were running down her face. "The woman who was the front seat passenger was killed."

Billy closed his eyes. He hated to see his mother crying, but now he understood why his parents had seemed so distressed when he had come round.

Oh no! he thought. Oh no! Not killed. I couldn't have killed somebody!

His slide into despair was speeded up by the next piece of news he heard. "And as if that wasn't enough," his mother was continuing, thinking that she'd better get it all over at once. "The woman in the car was eight months pregnant and her baby is dead too."

This was catastrophic.

How was Billy Morgan ever going to walk down the street in Ballymena again? His leg was broken, his pelvis was fractured and his eye was damaged, although not as badly as he had feared at first. He hadn't lost it. If he had though, and the mother and her baby had been spared, he probably wouldn't have cared so much.

Fear and revulsion took hold of the heart that was racing and thumping in Billy Morgan's battered chest. A lady and her unborn child were both dead, and all because of his stupidity.

If only she had lived and he had died. He would gladly now have given his life for hers. Or why could he not just have been killed as well? That would have been a relief, he thought. Then he would not have to do what he was going to be forced to do now. That was face up to dreadful disgrace and disgust of it all.

The next few months in hospital were a period of slow physical healing and slow mental torture. Billy knew that his body was getting better, but his mind was in constant turmoil. Graphic images of a dead mother and her dead baby haunted him day and night.

When Billy was eventually discharged from hospital four months later he was changed forever. With the setting of the bones in his leg, and the damage to his pelvis, one leg was shorter than the other and the sight of his right eye would be permanently impaired. He could live with these physical disabilities, however, well aware that they had been self-inflicted. The psychological scars would remain with him for as long as he lived. It seemed that they would never go away.

To make an already horrible situation totally horrendous Billy was discharged from the UDR following his release from hospital. With such a bashed-up body he was considered to be unfit for service with the rigours of the regiment and so was forced to add unemployment to his growing list of woes.

His conscience still tormented him, twenty-four hours a day, but he thought that when the court case about his accident came up he would probably be charged with dangerous driving and be put in jail. He actually looked forward to that. Whatever sentence the judge handed down he would be happy to serve. And the more severe it was the better. If he were compelled to serve a custodial sentence he would feel that he had at least in some way paid the price for his crime.

It was a year before the case was brought before the courts and when it did the charge brought against Billy was reduced from dangerous driving to careless driving.

He was fined £200 and didn't even lose his licence.

This wasn't justice, for him. Many would think he had escaped lightly, but he didn't. Billy Morgan had wanted to pay a high price for what he had done, to try and ease his overwhelmingly guilty conscience, and he hadn't been required to do that.

He felt cheated. Not only had he caused the death of a mother and her baby by his wanton recklessness but now he considered that he hadn't even been suitably punished for it.

How could he live with the shame?

3

IRELAND'S STRONGEST MAN?

FOLLOWING HIS DISCHARGE from hospital, all Billy wanted to do was find some way of avoiding people. He wished that he could become a recluse, not having to meet anybody or speak to anybody. If he could manage this he imagined that he could possibly survive, in a self-imposed isolation of ignominy.

Unaware of the full extent of his son's revulsion at himself, and desire to escape from society, Billy's father made a suggestion that was to provide him with a lifeline. He thought that Billy ought to join a gym. This, he said, would help strengthen his body after all that had happened, and it would also maybe even help stretch the bones in his shorter leg. In any event it would take him out of the house, and provide him with a focus in life.

After he had made a few enquiries he gave his struggling son the name of a gym and Billy went to see it. On arriving at the address the would-be new member had to climb a set of outside stairs, like a fire escape, and push open a heavy door. When he did so, he was greeted by a distinctive heavy smell, which he was later to discover had two main constituents, sweat and embrocation.

What exactly was going on in this place?

He wasn't left to wonder for long, though. Within minutes a tall, strong, fit- looking man had emerged through another door and offered to show him around.

Before he left again, three-quarters of an hour later, Billy had signed up to join the gym. During his conducted tour Billy had seen a number of grim-faced muscular men in singlets and shorts sweating profusely as they pumped away at weights or toiled away doggedly at strange-looking metal contraptions of all shapes and sizes. It wasn't the prospect of spending hours engaged in intensive physical training that influenced Billy to join up at the gym. It was the posture of the guy who had shown him around. He held himself so straight, and looked so confident in his superbly-proportioned body that Billy thought, 'If I can end up like that, I'm certainly willing to give it a go.'

After the first few weeks becoming acclimatised to the gym work and routine Billy began to actually enjoy the experience. It was quickly to become to him like a lifebelt thrown to a drowning man.

The supreme attraction of the gym was that Billy Morgan, shattered by shame, could hide there. He didn't have to associate with people if he didn't want to. Bodybuilding, on which he had become very keen, was an individual activity, and not a team sport. All he had to do was torture himself to lift heavier weights, turn in better times and develop bigger muscles. The pleasure of it all was in the pain of it all.

Billy was soon a keen bodybuilder. He was training vigorously four days a week and after he had been doing this for some time his instructor came to him one day with a proposition. "You are doing well on this programme, Billy," he began. "I believe you have potential. How would you feel about entering a bodybuilding contest?"

"I would like to, if you think I'm ready for it," was Billy's immediate and enthusiastic response. It was an exciting challenge. He was, at last, being offered the chance to recover some self-esteem. It was pleasing to be recognised as actually having the ability to excel at something. He sent off his entry form and trained even harder, constantly pushing himself to the limit of his physical ability.

The contest was held in the King's Hall, on the outskirts of Belfast in September 1976 and out of 23 competitors in his class, Billy came second. He was runner-up to the champion and he had only been involved in the sport for six months!

This provided the once self-deprecating Billy with a tremendous psychological boost. He could actually succeed at something, and the sport in which he had begun to shine was one in which he could endure, or perhaps even enjoy, as much physical punishment as he cared to inflict upon himself.

It was as he continued to maintain his interest in bodybuilding, and regain some measure of self-respect, that Billy met Katrina and they decided to get married. The wedding was in June 1977 and the couple's first baby, Paul, was born the following year. As a husband and father Billy decided that it was time to try and put his past, with all its haunting memories, behind him and make a fresh start.

When he started work in the huge Gallaher's tobacco factory outside Ballymena, and then bought a house in the town, he felt that he had turned the corner into Happiness Street.

The crowning achievement for Billy came in September 1980 when he competed in an all-Ireland bodybuilding contest in Dublin. He beat off stiff opposition to win the event and be acclaimed as Ireland's Strongest Man. Fame came with this title and soon Billy was being invited to do shows and demonstrations at venues all over the island and beyond.

Things were looking up.

Billy began to feel that perhaps life wasn't so bad after all. It wasn't to last, however.

Soon after winning the title, and just as he was beginning to enjoy his status as Ireland's Strongest Man, Billy began to feel ill. It started off with pains in his joints but when he began passing blood a few weeks later he became alarmed and went to his GP. Billy was admitted to the Waveney Hospital immediately, and tests were started in an effort to find out what was causing his problems.

Results were long in coming and as Billy lay in hospital he began losing weight rapidly. The muscular 85-kilogram frame was reduced to a pathetic 35-kilogram figure in a matter of months.

Billy thought he was going to die. What was wrong with him? The uncertainty was intolerable. If only he knew. His condition continued to worsen. One day when his wife and one of his friends came up to visit him he couldn't concentrate enough to make sensible conversation with them. They appeared like talking shadows beside his bed.

After extensive tests the medical staff came to a final diagnosis. Billy was told that he had Crone's disease and that there was no cure for it. The only treatment they could prescribe, to possibly ease the discomfort, was anti-inflammatory steroids.

For the next two years Billy was in and out of hospital constantly. He was unable to work, and being around the house all the time when not in hospital put a strain on his marriage.

Two years after he first took ill the doctors responsible for his case informed Billy that the only way back to anything resembling normal health for him was to have a permanent colostomy performed.

The operation took place in March 1983,and although having his bowel removed was the only medical solution to Billy's problem, he felt desolate after it had been done. He became obsessed with the impression that he wasn't now a complete person any more, that somehow his already mangled body had been mutilated even further.

When discharged from hospital he found it difficult to cope with the constraints of this new way of life. His problems were even further compounded when his wife, who had found all her husband's illness and hospitalisation more that she could manage to live with, and Billy, decided to separate. Katrina remained in the family home with little Paul, and he moved out.

Deep depression set in. Over a period of three years, Billy had lost his wife, his son and his home. One of Ireland's most muscular men had become one of Ireland's most miserable men.

At his wit's end once more, Billy reverted to bodybuilding, the sport that had provided him with such a welcome escape hatch after the accident nearly eight years before. On his return to the gym he met, and began training with, a Scottish bodybuilder who had come over to be an instructor in Ballymena.

This new friend recommended that Billy should start using oral and injectable steroids to improve his performance. Billy wanted to succeed more than anything, so he listened to that advice and began using performance-enhancing drugs on a regular basis. It would be great, he thought, to be back to his former glory. Could he win the Ireland's Strongest Man competition for a second time? Was it possible, even with the restraints that had now become part of his daily life?

It was, he reckoned, and it would give him something to work for, and something worth paying any price to achieve.

The steroids he had begun to use were expensive, however, and he was out of work. Where was he to find the money to pay for them?

Again the Scottish trainer had the answer.

"Why not sell some steroids to a few friends?" he urged. "That is the easiest, and quickest way of funding your own supply."

When Billy started to do this he found that it was true. It was an easy way to make ready money.

What he didn't consider, or even care about, was that he had begun, albeit in a small way, to deal in illegal drugs.

4

HAVE A DAB OF THIS

THERE WERE TWO other men at the gym club with whom Billy became friendly at that time. Harold and Brendan were like him in that they were willing to push themselves to any lengths to win competitions. In February 1984 all three of them went to compete in the Mr. Britain contest and Billy won an award for the most outstanding achievement by a British body-builder.

Billy and Brendan became close friends and began to party a lot with some others from the gym, especially at the weekends.

It was on one of these weekend trips that Billy found his travelling companions passing a brown envelope containing a white powder around in a car. There were five of them crammed into the vehicle and they were on their way to spend the evening, and probably the most of the night, at a club in Portrush on the north Antrim coast.

"Have a dab of this, Billy," the man beside him said. "It will make you feel good. Set you up for the night." Billy hesitated for a moment, so the guy with the envelope went on to demonstrate how it was done. He simply licked his finger, dabbed it into the powder, and then licked the powder off his damp finger with obvious relish. It reminded Billy of how he used to enjoy a bag of sherbet as a child.

Reckoning that if it were all right for the others in the car to be 'having a dab' it would be O.K. for him too, Billy licked his finger and stuck it into the bag. On pulling it out he had a look to make sure that it was covered in powder, and then he put it in his mouth.

He had just been introduced to 'speed.'

There was a certain amount of truth in what the fellow who had encouraged him to try it had said. The powder gave him a very pleasant floating-away feeling, completely different from the effect of alcohol, which had been his chief tool for escaping from reality, up until then.

It was significant, though, that the man who had suggested that he take a lick of the powder hadn't specified any time scale for its magic effect. Billy felt rotten the next day. Not only did he have a hangover, but he was also very depressed. Since depression wasn't by any means a new experience for Billy he thought nothing of it. Nor did he ever associate it with the powder from the night before.

There would only be one way to remedy the situation and that would be to have more next weekend. He did, too. And the next weekend, and the next. Then his mates persuaded him to experiment with 'some new experiences.' Within four or five months Billy had started to use LSD and cannabis, in addition to the amphetamines with which he had started off.

At this stage, though, he was only dabbling in drugs at the weekend. During the week he was so intent on his bodybuilding training that nothing could be allowed to deflect him from achieving the performance targets he had set himself.

In 1986 Billy met up with Katrina and they decided to come together again. Billy vowed to turn his back on his gym friends and the partying lifestyle and the pair settled under the same roof once more. Their daughter Laura was born a year later and Billy thought that he was on the road to a life of contentment and family bliss this time.

That, too, is how it appeared for the next three years. Billy returned to his job in Gallaher's factory and then, using his contacts in bodybuilding and his expertise in the sport, he set up his own gym in Antrim. Enthusiasts in the town were glad of this new facility and business began to build up.

Then, just when life seemed to be getting better by the month, misfortune struck again.

In 1989 Billy was involved in an accident at work. A steam pipe, which he had been working beside, burst, and he was badly burnt from his waist to his knees. He was rushed into the Waveney Hospital yet another time. It was nine weeks before his burns were sufficiently healed for him to be discharged, and when he did eventually get out Katrina had gone again. She had probably decided that Billy was one of the most unreliable men any woman could wish to have in her life. She was certainly tired of the constant running up and down to hospital with two young children. Having considered these matters she concluded that she could give Paul and Laura more attention, and provide them with a more stable home environment on her own.

And so she moved out, taking the two children with her.

When Billy arrived home he was on his own, once more. Where did he go from here?

He went back to the life he had been determined to leave, the world of pubs, clubs and partying. There seemed to be little else to live for. Billy would be unable to work for quite some time and so he had time on his hands and little to do but reflect on his woes.

One evening in a bar he met a man and his girlfriend, both of whom seemed friendly. They were travelling people and had interesting stories to tell. Billy liked their open geniality and the three of them began to meet up on a regular basis.

A few months later the pair married and moved in with Billy. Now he had company in the house, and that company attracted other company. Soon all three of them were going out somewhere, or having someone in with them, every night of the week.

Billy was back to his old ways. He was slipping, without even stopping to give it a thought, deeper and deeper into an incessant round of drinking and using drugs.

Nor did the knowledge of what was going on around him cause him any sense of guilt or revulsion, either.

An example of this occurred when he had been out for a drink with some friends one evening and was on his way to a drugs party. On their way to the house in the Doury Road estate in Ballymena where the party was to be held, Billy and his friends stopped to have a chat with a couple of girls they knew.

They were just about to part and go their separate ways when they saw a young man staggering towards them. He was making strange noises. As he stumbled below a streetlamp Billy and his friends could see that there was blood spurting from his chest. They knew straightaway what had happened. He had been stabbed.

Suddenly the young man slumped sideways over the bonnet of a parked car.

Then in spectacular, almost stage-managed slow motion, the blood-soaked body slid slowly off the front of it, to end up in a crumpled heap on the road.

He was dead.

Were Billy and his crowd upset?

No. They just shrugged their shoulders and thought, what has he been up to? Probably had it coming to him.

Did they ring the police to report what looked like a murder?

No way. They had no desire to tangle with the police. Policemen asked too many questions.

Somebody would likely contact them sometime. They had other things to do. Billy and his friends went on to the party, which lasted all night.

When they came out next morning the body had gone.

That wasn't an isolated incident, either.

At other times Billy had seen people who had overdosed being left to die, alone. Or dealers shot dead over payments or territory.

The man, who had once been so sensitive, had become totally desensitised.

Nothing seemed to matter. Life was cheap, but drugs were dear. And getting the next fix was all that mattered.

Billy's habit was to make more pressing demands on his resourcefulness, too, after an experience he had in an old shed at the back of an empty house in the Doury Road. His traveller friend had bought some crack cocaine and between them they made a crude pipe and started to smoke the drug.

This was something new and different for Billy, again.

He liked the feeling it gave him.

What he found more appealing was that he had discovered another means by which to escape from the phantoms of the past, and the endless pointlessness of the present.

Soon an old problem began to raise its head once more. It was the dicey matter of funding this latest addiction.

Crack cocaine was expensive stuff.

To buy more and more of it was going to take more and more money.

This presented Billy Morgan with a crucial challenge.

How was he going to come by the cash?

5

THE CURIOUS CLAW

IN THE SHADY underworld where Billy operated there was only one way to make big money fast.

That was to start doing deliveries for the drug dealers. They were trading in huge sums and if Billy could only do a few 'drops' for them he could probably make enough to pay for his habit.

He let it be known that he was available and the person from whom he bought his 'gear' introduced him to a notorious dealer. This man had many contacts and anybody prepared to risk working for him could usually find himself well off. That was of course, provided that he worked according to certain unwritten, but well-understood rules.

Billy began doing a few 'errands' for him and with the money he made, and the drugs readily available, continued to advance his addictions. With the contacts he made in his new 'job' Billy was invited to more parties in different places and at one of these he met a young woman he found attractive.

This girl was only 19 years old at the time and in the course of conversation Billy told her that he was due to deliver a load of steroids to a gym in Dublin the following day.

"Can I come with you?" Em asked, eagerly. "I would love a run to Dublin."

"I don't see why not," Billy replied, feeling rather flattered that such a vibrant young woman should want to accompany him, a man nearly twice her age, to Dublin for the day.

That was to be the start of what promised to be a lasting friendship. As Billy and Em set out for Dublin the next morning they discovered that they had similar interests. Chief amongst these seemed to be an apparently insatiable desire for drink, drugs and wild parties.

Em moved in to live with Billy a few weeks later and they began to enjoy themselves. Their tastes were expensive, however, and Billy could not make the amount of money they were going through every week by doing a few deliveries for the drug dealers. Other solutions would have to be sought.

The first of these was to sell the house they were living in, and move into a Housing Executive house on the Ballykeel estate in the town. Having obtained £50,000 for the house, Billy had a ready reserve at the 'hole-in-the-wall', and he made use of it. He and Em were spending more that £500 a week to subsidise their hectic lifestyle. As they began to see the bottom of Billy's 'pot of gold' Em chipped in with her contribution. She was awarded £17,000 as settlement for an injury claim following a hit-and-run accident and it went 'into the kitty.' This helped keep them in drugs and booze for a while, but as they had both begun using crack cocaine regularly, it was soon 'blown' also.

When what seemed at one time to be an endless supply of ready cash actually dried up, the relationship became more tense. There were frequent arguments. Billy and Em, who had once travelled the country together, revelling in a life of overpriced addiction, were now forced to steal the food they needed to keep alive.

They began to blame each other for the predicament they found themselves in. The compelling cry of their bodies for a 'fix', and the lack of any resources to buy it, led to irritation and acrimony.

The relationship eventually came to a slow and torturous end. Maintaining that he 'couldn't put up with it any longer,' Billy moved out and his traveller friends in the Doury Road took him in.

As he was now a confirmed heroin addict he was forced to return to doing 'jobs' for the dealers to buy his 'gear.' It was a violent, volatile world in which to be living. One week Billy had met a dealer from Newry 'on business.' Next week he was to hear that the dealer's body had been found dumped somewhere. He had been shot in the head.

Having lived with his friends for some time Billy rented a flat of his own. Although it was good to have his own place Billy soon found that he was beset by two problems that never seemed to go away. What was worrying was that they just seemed to grow worse week by week.

The first of these was the old and ever-recurring question of finance. Any money he made for any 'jobs' he did, was spent on drugs. So he couldn't afford to buy furniture. The almost down-and-out had an old sofa he bought from a charity shop, a second-hand TV and a telephone, in case anybody had 'work' for him, and that was all. He slept in a sleeping bag on the floor of what was supposed to be the 'bed' room.

His other concern was physical and much more alarming. Billy recognised that the lack of amenities was the price he had to be prepared to pay in order to obtain the drugs he craved, but this was different.

It all began with numbness in his fingers. Soon Billy found that he was beginning to drop things. Over a period of time this lack of feeling in his hand and mobility in his fingers became so serious that he found he couldn't pick up even the lightest article without having to concentrate intensely on the exercise. Then, after all the effort, he was liable to drop the picked-up object almost at once, as he had lost the ability to close his hand in anything like an effective grip.

This lack of power in his hands, which had begun to worry Billy deeply, came to a frightening climax one morning in June 2002. He woke up to find that he could not move his left hand at all. It was locked in a weird position. The thumb was turned in and pressing onto the palm of his hand. The index and middle fingers were stuck out straight, pointing forward in powerless, motionless paralysis. The remaining two fingers were bent in over, and pressing tightly upon, the thumb, wedging it firmly into position against the palm. And nothing moved.

Billy Morgan's hand had become like something out of a monster movie, like a curious, cruel, crooked claw.

It was scary. Billy realised that it was time he had medical attention for this complaint, whatever it was. He rang his traveller friends and when they heard how annoyed he was they volunteered to take him to the Accident and Emergency Unit in Antrim Area Hospital.

When a doctor had examined Billy he was told that when a specialist had seen him and assessed his case they would decide where he could be admitted to receive appropriate attention.

As Billy lay wondering what was going to happen next a young man whom he knew from the Doury Road in Ballymena was wheeled in. He had been a heroin addict and had obviously overdosed.

There was a flurry of activity by a doctor and some nurses around the trolley for a few minutes then it all subsided. A sheet was pulled up over the patient's head and the trolley was wheeled away.

It had all been too late.

The lad had died.

Billy was suddenly gripped by an overwhelming sense of fear and dread.

If this curious claw that he had once known as his left hand was nothing more than an outward symptom of some inward incurable disease, what would happen to him?

Was he going to die, too?

The prospect struck terror in his heart.

If he was going to die, he wasn't ready to die.

There were certain things he knew he would have to get sorted.

And fast.

6

PREPARED TO DIE?

"YOU ARE BEING transferred to Musgrave Park for further tests," was the decision of the doctors when it came, delivered to Billy by a senior member of the nursing staff.

"That's O.K." was the response from the bed. Musgrave Park Hospital in Belfast, Billy knew, was a leading centre for the treatment of orthopaedic conditions. He could only accept that the doctors who had examined him must have considered that it would be the most suitable hospital to look into the strange case of the helpless hand.

Before the nurse moved away, Billy asked her if he could have a phone brought up to the side of his bed. If his condition was as dreadful as he feared, he would need to make contact with his two children and let them know. He recognised that it would be quite shocking for them if he went into Musgrave Park Hospital and died, without them ever having known he was ill. It would be only fair to prepare them for the worst.

Having fumbled to use the payphone with the only hand he had left that worked, Billy rang the house in Ballymena where the children were living with their mum.

It was Laura he spoke to first.

"Hello, love," Billy began, the joy of speaking to the daughter who was one of the bright lights in his drab existence, was somewhat overshadowed by the impending sense of doom that had overtaken him.

When Laura had replied, "Oh hello dad, where are you?" Billy proceeded to tell her where he was, and how he felt. "I am in Antrim Hospital, waiting to be transferred to the Musgrave. There is something wrong with my hand. It is all twisted up and I can't move it. I am afraid there may be something really serious the matter with me."

He paused before carrying on with what was the real thrust of his message, his chief reason for ringing. "I just want you to know, Laura, that I love you, and I want to say that I'm sorry for having been such a useless father to you. If I ever get better and am out of hospital again I promise to come and see you more often and do everything I possibly can for you."

After he had finished telling Laura how much she meant to him, Billy then spoke to Paul and told him much the same. If he were never to see them again he wanted to make sure that his children knew how precious they had been to him. They told him that they loved him, too, and not to worry. They were sure somebody in the hospital in Belfast would be able 'to sort him out.'

Billy found it hard to share their confidence. When he had put the phone down he lay wondering how long he had left to live.

Were his addictions to blame for the state he was in?

Or was this payback time for the accident? The feeling of gathering gloom was made even darker by searing pangs of guilt and shame. If he hadn't considered himself punished severely enough by the law, was he going to have to suffer for the untimely death of a mother and her unborn baby, by going to an early grave?

Any other form of retribution he could have faced, but Billy could not bear the thought of having to pay the ultimate price. This was not because he didn't think he deserved it, but because he knew that he was not prepared for it.

He trembled at the thought of dying, but he had no choice in the matter. If this paralysis that had struck his hand was related to some terrible incurable condition, maybe something in his brain, then he was set to die, without a doubt.

His past would have caught up with him at last.

Later that day an ambulance came to take Billy to Musgrave Park Hospital where his condition was to be monitored from day to day. He was kept in hospital during the week and allowed home at the weekends. His brother collected him on Friday afternoon and brought him back on Monday morning. It became a regular pattern, but with the lack of any improvement in his condition, and the constant taking of drugs to ease the increasing pain in all his joints without any final diagnosis as to what was the cause of it all, Billy remained very depressed.

In hospital he was denied access to heroin and crack cocaine but was given morphine and diazepam for his physical and mental complaints. This meant that the autumn he was to spend in and out of hospital didn't cure him of his drug dependency. It merely changed it, from existing as a craving for recreational drugs to a reliance on prescription drugs.

He wasn't getting any better, though, and this was distressing.

Were they just keeping him running back and forward to hospital until something dreadful happened and then that would be it? If that was going to be the case there was another matter which had to be dealt with. It was something that he had forgotten about when he was well enough, but now that he had become obsessed with this idea that he was going to die, he needed to put it right.

The opportunity to do so came one Saturday afternoon in his flat in Ballymena. His mother had called round to see him, and there was nobody else with him at the time.

As they chatted about general matters the conversation came around to events that had happened within the family circle over the previous two or three decades. It was when they were reminiscing about the life and death of different relatives that Billy seized his opportunity.

"Do you remember that St. Patrick's night when Billy Kenny was murdered?" he began by way of an opener.

His mum nodded. "Indeed I do. How could I ever forget it?" she replied, just a little puzzled.

"Well there is something I want to tell you about that night," her son continued. "Billy made me promise that I wouldn't tell anybody, so I didn't. I have never breathed a word of it for the past 30 years, for not only did I swear to Billy that I wouldn't, but I also thought that it might be awkward for his wife and parents to take at the time. Most of them are now either dead and gone, or scattered all over the place, so I think it will be O.K. to tell you, and it would probably be a good idea if you were to tell the police."

A shadow crossed his mother's face, but Billy chose to ignore it and went on, "When Billy lifted me to take me from York Street Station to the boat that night there was a young woman in the car. I haven't a clue who she was or what she was doing with Billy. All I know is that she was there, and that Billy asked me not to say a word about her to anybody. Even when the police came over to question me in England I didn't tell them, but I'm sure it wouldn't do any harm to let them know now."

"No. I can't see that it would," his mother agreed. "Sure they arrested two young boys for Billy's murder and they went to jail for it. They will be out again by now."

It was true, and Billy was relieved to have finally shared his long-and-loyally-kept secret with someone. He had visited

Ballymena police station dozens of times, for all kinds of reasons, during his colourful career, but had never felt it right to 'spill the beans' about his cousin. Now that his mother had undertaken to 'tell them sometime' he felt as though a burden had been lifted from his shoulders.

That was always one thing less to worry about. At least if whatever it was that was wrong with him, killed him, then he wouldn't have carried his secret to the grave.

In early December, Billy was told that he would be allowed home for four days over the Christmas period. The prospect brought him no joy. He had come to the stage that nothing brought him any joy. He was living in constant fear, and appeared permanently depressed. His hand was no better and he imagined that other parts of his body were seizing up as well.

When his brother brought him back to his flat on December 23 Billy had only two things in his mind to do over the holiday period. One was a definite plan for something he couldn't miss doing, as a token of his love. The other was something that he had begun to consider seriously over the previous few weeks, as an escape from all this misery of uncertainty, an act of desperation.

On Christmas Eve he put plan one into action. He went down the town in Ballymena and bought a present each for Paul and Laura. Having had these gifts suitably wrapped by shop assistants he then took them round and gave them to the two children. They were glad to see their dad out of hospital and thanked him so much for his kindness, little knowing what he was contemplating doing when he left them.

Billy's shopping trip that afternoon had included more than presents for the two kids. He had also bought a collection of tablets and a bottle of vodka.

When he arrived back to his flat, desolate and depressed, he spent a restless night considering his next move. He had become convinced that life had nothing left for him, and that his physical condition was only set to grow worse until he became totally paralysed and then eventually died in agony.

From midnight until one or two in the morning was a terrible time. It was 27 years ago to the hour since his drunken driving accident and it came up before him as though it had only happened 27 minutes before. It all came up on the screen of his mind so vividly. The smell of petrol. The red paint. No windscreen. Trapped legs. Voices in the night...

The words 'she's dead Billy, and so is her unborn baby,' echoed in his ears...

Could he live with the shame?

No.

The thought that had been impressing itself upon him with greater urgency over the past while, and certainly that night, was that if he couldn't live with the shame, why did he have to live at all? Why not just die? Just as his victims had done.

And when would be a better time to end all the speculation about the future, and all the conscience about the past, than Christmas morning?

Just as children all around the town were awakening to the excitement of Christmas, Billy Morgan decided to end all the anguish forever.

He settled himself on the settee, and swallowed the collection of tablets he had bought the day before, certain that they would do the trick. These he washed down with frequent gulps of vodka from his bottle.

As he lay gazing up at the light, waiting for the tablets to take effect, and life to ebb from his body, Billy was overtaken by a strange sense of peace and purpose. This was the answer. He was going, going, going... Wherever he was going, he was going, going, going...

Billy Morgan wakened up, later that day in Antrim Area Hospital, dismayed to discover that he hadn't actually gone. Two friends had called, for some reason that they were at a loss to explain, to see Billy that morning, and sensing that something was wrong had broken in and found him slumped unconscious on the settee. They had rushed him to the A&E unit in the hospital where he had been resuscitated.

When the staff in Antrim were satisfied that he was well enough to be moved they transferred him back to Musgrave Park. And the medical team there definitely weren't going to let him out again.

His Christmas holiday was over and his suicide attempt had been thwarted, but what was going to happen to him now?

7

YOU ARE IN BIG TROUBLE

EARLY IN JANUARY a young surgeon came and stood beside Billy's bed. He had the air of a man on a mission, and Billy was glad to see him. It would be good to have news of any kind on his condition, and hopefully there would be some relief from the nagging worry about what was ultimately going to happen to him.

"Well doctor, what's the news?" he enquired, trying not to appear over anxious.

"The news is, Billy," the surgeon came straight to the point, "that you are in big trouble." By the jaunty manner in which this pronouncement was made, and given that the speaker had a smile playing around at the edges of his mouth, Billy thought he was joking.

"Come on, tell me the truth, are you joking or not? How big is big?" the worried patient continued.

Recognising that Billy was keen to know the whole truth about the cause of his paralysed hand, the surgeon went on in more sombre tone, "I mean it, Billy, and I'm not joking. You are in big trouble. And big is very big. The upper part of your spine has collapsed, probably from using all the steroids you have been taking during your bodybuilding days, and is pressing against your spinal cord. That is what is causing the problem with your hand. You are going to need intensive surgery to relieve the pressure, and this will have to be done in two parts."

Billy sat listening intently to what he was being told. At last he knew the cause of the curious claw, but what would the remedy entail? Surgery, in two parts. What did that mean? The surgeon had the answer.

"In the first stage we will take a bone from your pelvis and then cut across your throat to allow us to place that bone between the vertebrae," he explained. "When that is complete you will be given some time to recover before we go in a second time. Then it will be to open up the back of your skull and insert two rods, just like knitting needles. These will be placed down through the vertebrae and then fixed to the base of the skull. When in position they will strengthen and stabilise your spine."

It all sounded rather complicated, and not a little scary. Billy had heard of people having their throats cut and their skulls split before, but never on an operating table. The images the words conjured up for him came straight out of the mental picture book of his violent past.

"There are difficulties involved with this procedure that I have to warn you about," the surgeon went on, "and one of these is a permanent after-effect. You will have no movement in the upper part of your spine. It will be completely stiff and inflexible."

Billy was just about to say, "That won't really matter as long as my hand is fixed and I don't get any worse," but he didn't get the chance.

The surgeon was in full flow outlining the possible complications that could occur during the two operations, and in the interim waiting period. He then concluded his synopsis with the blunt truth. "I wouldn't worry about all this stuff, if I were you," he said. " The operations carry with them such a high degree of risk you probably won't survive them anyway."

Having explained very fully both the cause of Billy's complaint and the risks involved in the curing of it, the surgeon left it with Billy. "Some surgeons would not even undertake this operation as it is so risky," he declared. " But from all the information I have before me I can see that it is your only chance of ever returning to anything near normality and I am willing to do it for you. The final choice must rest with you, though. It is up to you if you want to go ahead."

It didn't take Billy long to make up his mind. The prospects of having his hand, and sense of touch and power to grip back to normal, far outweighed any difficulties that could possibly lie ahead. And what if there was a chance that he wouldn't survive? Had he not tried to end all the misery a month ago, and failed? If he died on the operating table, so what?

Having been given Billy's approval to proceed and make the necessary arrangements the surgeon told him that he would have to be transferred to the spinal unit in the nearby Royal Victoria Hospital to have the operation. He would be notified when everything was agreed and in place.

All he could do now was wait, and during this in-between period Billy remained in Musgrave Park Hospital during the week and was allowed to spend the weekends in his flat in Ballymena. Most of his former friends, but not all, had forgotten about him. One of the few who thought about Billy from time to time was Harold Penney, a companion and fellow-competitor from his bodybuilding days.

Having made a few enquiries as to his whereabouts Harold called one Saturday afternoon to visit Billy and was shocked to see the state he was in. The man who had once been acclaimed as Ireland's Strongest Man had been reduced to little more than a wasted weakling. His face was pale and pitted and lined with anxiety. An oddly twisted hand was the predominant feature of the shapeless tangle that had once been a firm body and powerful limbs. Lying listlessly on the settee, where he was when Harold first saw him, he looked like someone who had neither the interest nor the ability to struggle up from that recumbent position.

Harold's instinctive reaction was to go straight across to where Billy was, and as he sat down beside him big tears trickled down his cheeks.

"I never thought that Billy Morgan would ever end up looking like this," he said, obviously touched.

Billy was pleased to see his former friend again and as they began to talk over old times he appreciated the warmth of Harold's approach. He had always been a caring sort of person, but now there seemed to be something different about him. Harold now appeared genuinely concerned for his once-upon-a-time bodybuilding buddy in more than merely the physical sense and the reason for this concern was soon to manifest itself.

In the course of conversation Harold told Billy that he had become a Christian some time before and that God had turned his life around completely. He now claimed to be a totally new and very much happier person, with a definite goal in life and no fear of death. As a kind of proof of the wonder of this changed lifestyle which he had now embraced, he went on to say that his wife, who had once been very ill, was now healed because many Christians 'from all over the country' had been praying for her.

What surprised Billy most about Harold's story of his conversion, as he had called it once, was that the main purpose of telling him all about it was that he would be well advised to consider it seriously too. The benefits, according to Harold, were not only for this life, but also for something called 'eternity,' which Billy gathered was what he had always called the 'hereafter,' and meant forever and ever and ever.

There were two things about Harold that Billy found appealing during that visit. The first was the transformation that had taken place in his life, and the other was his sincerity about his Christianity.

There could be no doubting the conviction in his voice as he said, "Billy, I believe God has a plan for your life. He has made a new man out of me, and He can do the very same for you, if only you will trust in Him."

When it came time for Harold to go, he assured Billy that he would 'be praying for him' and let himself out to save the miserable man on the sofa having to rise. As the sound of footsteps grew fainter and farther away Billy thought, 'Dear help Harry. He means well. But imagine coming to tell somebody like me who could be dead in a couple of months, that God has a plan for his life! The truth of the matter is that the last thing I think I need at this moment in time is somebody coming in to preach to me!'

Harold's visit had made an impression, though, without Billy having been actually aware of it. It had introduced the idea of God, and a life after death, into the mind of someone who, if the doctor's predictions were to be believed, was more likely to be dead that alive in six months time.

It was April 2003, and a few weeks later, when back in hospital, Billy was sorting through a pile of magazines that had been left on a table in the ward. As he did so he came upon a booklet of Daily Bread Bible Readings and began to leaf through it.

The frequent mention of the word 'God' in it attracted his attention. This God thing had been gnawing away at him since Harold's call that Saturday afternoon. Maybe this little book would throw some light on the subject. At least he could read it without feeling that he was being 'got at.' If it didn't make any sense to him he could leave it down.

Taking it over to his bedside chair Billy began to read some of the articles in the booklet more carefully. It was a back number but Billy wasn't interested in matching a reading to a date. All he wanted to know was what it had to say about God, and if it mentioned anything at all about this peace and satisfaction that Harold had been on about. Could it possibly explain whatever it was that had changed his life?

There was a story on the very last page that intrigued Billy. He read it over twice, for the state of the man described in it bore remarkable resemblances to his situation. This person had been in a diving accident and was paralysed. In hospital, and fearing for his life he had closed his eyes one day and asked God to give him peace and assurance. God heard his plea and the patient was able to live more positively in the days that followed, as all fear of death had been removed.

Billy found this page compelling. He read it over a few more times. Could God do the same for him as He had done for the guy in the story? he began to wonder.

Later that evening, with a pervading God-consciousness having begun to dominate all his thinking, Billy lay back and closed his eyes. He began to pray, although he did not recognise what he was doing as praying. As far as he was concerned he was merely talking a few things over with God.

"Please God don't let me die," he began sincerely. "I'm sorry for the life I have led and all the bad things I have done and I'm scared about what lies ahead." Words began to flow more easily as he continued to pour out his heart in confession and contrition, "Please, I am asking You to accept me and help me to live the way I ought to live and the way You want me to live. Whatever it takes, I'll do it. If You are real, God, just save me now and I will serve You for the rest of my life, however long that may be."

After asking God to accept him as he was, Billy felt a strange sense of peace come over him. It were as though all the burdens of his past and all the fears for the future had silently decided to slink away out of his mind, leaving it ready to entertain an even more comforting package of God-thoughts.

Billy recognised that something in him, or about him, had changed. He couldn't explain it. All he could be certain about was that it had happened.

The proof that a tangible transformation of some kind had taken place in his life came a day or two later when his parents came up to visit him. As they were about to leave his bedside to set out on the return journey to Ballymena, Billy's mother asked, "Is there anything else you think you need? Anything you want us to bring you?"

"Yes. As a matter of fact there is," Billy replied. Mother's question had afforded him the opportunity to ask for something that he had become convinced he needed to get his hands on as soon as possible. "I wonder if, next time you are coming, you could bring me a Bible?" he enquired.

"Certainly," was the immediate response. "There ought to be one about the house somewhere, and if there isn't we will buy you one and bring it up. Don't worry, Billy, we will find you a Bible."

That was good. Billy was pleased for he now had a feeling that he could find out more about this wonderful, reassuring relationship he had with God, by reading the Bible.

Not having given his parents any reason for what they considered an unusual request from Billy, they had a different reaction entirely, however.

"Billy must be sure that he isn't going to survive this operation," mother observed anxiously to father as they walked out to the car park. "He must have a hunch that he is going to die. Did you hear him asking for a Bible?" Despite their misgivings they brought Billy a Bible on their next visit, and he derived great satisfaction from reading it, finding the stories of Jesus in the Gospels most uplifting.

A month later, in May 2003, Billy was transferred to the Royal Victoria Hospital to have the surgery performed on his spine. Although the surgeon had outlined the considerable risks involved in the procedure, Billy was surprised to find that he felt unusually relaxed at the prospect of it.

The night before he was due to go to theatre he lay and committed the operation, and his life, into the hands of God. "Please take care of me tomorrow, Lord," he prayed simply. "I am trusting You to bring me through. Please don't let me die."

That prayer was answered, for later the following day Billy woke up in the hospital's Intensive Care Unit. The initial, and potentially the more dangerous, part of the operation to place two rods in Billy's spine had been completed successfully.

Soon after he recovered consciousness Billy was beset by a most terrifying experience. He had been given so many painkilling drugs that he began to hallucinate. He felt that he was going to be tortured and then murdered. His mind was totally overwhelmed by images of himself being chased by violent, ruthless people who were threatening, in the most frightening language, to kill him and hack his body to pieces.

More than once during this turbulent period Billy became so distraught that he attempted to climb out of bed. He was convinced that he had to run away in an attempt to escape from the apparitions that were pursuing him, drawing ever closer, and were just about to murder him.

At one stage, in his frenzied, delirious state he started to yell at, and struggle with the hospital staff who were trying to restrain him, accusing them of beating him up! Their only response to such behaviour was to monitor the distressed patient's condition, fully aware that the drugs that were being administered would soon calm him down.

As this started to happen and Billy became less agitated, he lay motionless at last, reflecting on the images that had been afflicting his mind, pictures of brutal torture and violent death. Thinking over the significance of these impressions that had been so alarmingly lifelike, he became convinced that God was trying to teach him two lessons through them.

The first of these was that if his would-be attackers had been permitted to carry out all the threats they had bawled at him during his horrifying hallucinations then it would have been no less than he would have deserved. When he considered all the sins he had committed during his lifetime what else did he deserve but to be punished to the point of death?

Further contemplation brought him suddenly face to face with another stupefying fact. It hit him like a bolt from the blue. That was what it must have been like for Jesus. Billy had read the story of Jesus' trial and crucifixion many times over the past four or five weeks. And He was the Son of God who, having lived a totally sinless life on earth was bearing the punishment for the sins of the entire world in one battered, bruised and beaten human body.

It was a sobering, humbling thought. Jesus had to endure being forsaken by his friends and being taunted, tortured and murdered by His enemies all to pay the price of the sins he had committed in his earlier, wilder days.

"Thank you Lord, for dying for me," Billy whispered, as the full recognition of what it had cost Jesus to come to live on earth and then submit to the physical torment and divine retribution of Calvary dawned upon him.

This revelation of what it had been like for Jesus to suffer and die for him helped Billy through the next week, when he was expected to lie as still as possible on the flat of his back to allow sufficient healing to take place before the second stage of his operation could be attempted.

When the surgeon was satisfied that he was now fit for the next phase he performed the operation and Billy was to get a wonderful surprise as he began to recover after it. His hand, which had been little more that a twisted claw for almost a year, was now back to normal.

With the rods in his spine correcting his physical ailment, and a new spirit of God in his body giving him a sense of purpose in life that he had never experienced before, Billy was anxious to recover and be out of hospital as soon as possible. Within a week of his second phase operation he was asking the medical staff to reduce his painkilling drugs. He had spent years being bolstered by drugs and he was keen to be rid of them as soon as possible.

The surgeon had told him that he was in big trouble, and he had been right.

What Billy was to recognise in hospital, however, was that his big trouble hadn't just begun with his horrible hooked hand. He had been in big trouble all his life.

That April day though, when he had asked God to spare his life and accept him into His family, his troubled background had seemed to disappear over some distant horizon, and now he had so much to live for.

Billy Morgan had a lot of ground to make up.

8

ONE MORE HUG AND I'M OUT!

BEFORE THAT DAY in the hospital when Billy committed his life to Christ he had always harboured in his mind two vague images of what a Christian really was. These were totally different, as they were based on cursory, and contrasting past experiences, and Billy had never even been sufficiently interested to give either of them anything more that fleeting consideration.

The first image was that of someone who went to church at least once every Sunday and was willing to dive into pocket or purse to give a few items of loose change to the people who always seemed to be collecting for one good cause or another in the street.

That was all there was to it. Nod to God on a Sunday and be as kind as you could to as many people as you could for the rest of the week.

Another, and more complex, picture of Christianity came with the men in the dark suits and with the loud voices. These were the men who always seemed to be standing in a well-dressed arc in the bandstand in the centre of Ballymena every Saturday afternoon. They declared themselves to be Christians, in no uncertain terms, basing their claim on the fact that they had been 'born again.'

Billy had never doubted these men's sincerity. Some of them had the habit of getting really worked up about what they were saying as though they firmly believed it to be, as they maintained, 'a matter of life and death.' What annoyed Billy was the way in which they personalised and projected their beliefs to everyone within earshot.

Many a Saturday afternoon when he was on a pub-crawl with some of his mates Billy used to become annoyed to learn that if he wasn't 'saved' then he was 'a sinner on his way to hell.' When he was sober enough to pay any attention at all, he had, on a number of occasions found this allegation disturbing. He wasn't so worried about being dubbed 'a sinner', for he had never reckoned himself to be any paragon of virtue, but the bit about going to hell really got to him. This irritation was usually of short duration, though, for whenever he reached the next pub on the list for that afternoon and had downed another couple of pints he had forgotten all about it.

When he arrived home from hospital to a different flat, which his parents had procured and furnished for him, Billy began a completely new life in a different location. Not wishing to return to his old haunts, or have anything to do with his former companions he decided to remain in the flat as much as possible. His only forays into the outside world were either to buy food or attend a church service.

He had decided that he would like to live as a Christian of the donation to the charity box on Saturday, nodding acquaintance with church on Sunday, variety. This worked well for a while until Billy started to read his Bible every day and discover more and more Christian channels on TV. Then two things began to happen, very gradually, in his life.

One of these was thrilling. It was the realisation of the peace and satisfaction that could come from personal prayer. Having thought for years that praying was a ritual reserved only for ministers and priests, Billy found that this was not so. He learnt that he was a child of God and as such he could approach his Heavenly Father at anytime and praise Him for His goodness and pour out his requests before Him. This was wonderful and afforded Billy great comfort.

With continued Bible study, and an increasing interest in prayer, he also recognised that another desire was beginning to increase within him. It was the longing to find others who had similar interests as himself. There must be dozens of them out there, he thought. Just as he had once loved to be out drinking with the boys, now he yearned to be out celebrating his new life in Christ with others who wanted to do the same. It was true that he was going to church every Sunday morning and although he was hearing the Bible read and a sermon of sorts it wasn't satisfying the cravings of his God-hungry soul.

Where could he find people with the fire in their souls that he was beginning to feel burning in his? Were there any of them in Ballymena?

The answer to that question was to come after Clinton, a young man who had known Billy for many years, called to pay him a visit. Clinton was delighted to hear that Billy had become a Christian and invited the recent convert to come along with him to the evening service in Victory Praise, which was, he said, 'his church.'

Billy agreed to go, wondering if this was where he could find the kind of Christians he was looking for. He could now understand fully why the men at the bandstand had been so intense about the message they had been preaching, for he had now experienced the sense of peace and satisfaction 'that is to be found only in Christ,' that they had been talking about. He thought, though, that you had to be articulate enough to be able to stand and preach in the street to join that group, so he wouldn't seek them out in the meantime. Perhaps Victory Praise would be his scene, with an acceptable mix of charitable giving, public preaching and explaining a bit about the Bible.

The service in Victory Praise was to commence at six o'clock but Clinton was late calling to collect Billy and so when they arrived for the service the hall was almost full. As soon as they walked into the porch of the building a man came across to Billy, put his arms around him, gave him a hug and exclaimed, "Great to see you, brother! You are very welcome! Go on ahead on in there!"

When Billy was released from his clutches he went over to the door Clinton was holding open for him. He stepped nervously through it and another man, who had been showing people to their seats stepped forward, and whispered, "Nice to meet you," before hugging him again.

The welcome was enthusiastic, but Billy, who had never come across that kind of demonstrative Christian love in his life before, found it embarrassing. As he followed Clinton who was following the leader up to the front to find a seat he vowed silently, "If another man attempts to put his arms around me in this place I'm leaving. One more hug and I'm out!"

The service had just begun when Billy and Clinton were shown to two seats right in the middle of the front row. They couldn't have been any closer to the action, and what action! There were three guys with guitars on the platform just in front of them and they were playing and singing their hearts out. When the call came for the congregation to join in everybody stood up and people all round Billy started raising their arms in the air and holding them there.

So this was Victory Praise. This was Clinton's church.

He had whispered to Billy that the three young men on the platform were the 'worship leaders.' Now Billy was still at the stage of coming to terms with a whole new Christian vocabulary, trying to learn what was meant by a battery of church-type words. He wasn't quite sure yet what he understood by the word 'worship' but what he did know for certain was that the three young men performing with such zest and vigour just eight or ten yards in front of him didn't fit anywhere at all into the hazy picture he had of it. If I was only out of here, I will certainly never be back, he determined very early on in the proceedings.

Later in the meeting, when the pastor began to speak, Billy realised that this man had what seemed like a phenomenal knowledge of the Bible, and what was more, he seemed very keen to get his point across. What he couldn't understand, though, was that a lot of the people in the congregation seemed to feel that they had to do their little bit to help him on. Every now and again somebody would shout out "Hallelujah!" or "Praise the Lord!" or "Amen!" The 'Amen' one left Billy a bit puzzled. In the church he had been going to every Sunday morning since coming out of hospital they always said 'Amen' at the end of prayers, but never in the middle of sermons. Was this a message for the preacher to stop? He couldn't be sure.

When the service was over it took Billy and Clinton quite a while to make it out of the hall from their seat at the front. What Billy found strange as they filed out was that people he had never seen in his life before stopped to speak to him, and from little old grey-haired ladies to young guys in jeans the message was the same. They all claimed to be 'glad to see him.'

The silence in the car on the way home was more of the awkward than the sinister variety. Clinton obviously didn't want to ask Billy what he thought of Victory Praise, in case he would give him an honest answer. Billy, on the other hand didn't want to say anything that would offend the friend who had been good enough to take him along. The truth was that the whole thing had been too much of a Christian culture shock for him. To have been once was nice, but once would be enough. He hoped Clinton wouldn't ask him to go again as he was leaving him off at his door, and he didn't. What a relief! It saved him having to refuse.

Monday and Tuesday were spent in reflection. Billy began to think about Victory Praise and why he had found it so different from any church service he had ever been to before. The people were very friendly and had seemed genuinely interested in him. That was hardly a crime. Not only did they appear pleased to see him but they also seemed happy to be with one another and there could be no doubt about it they looked delighted to be praising the Lord.

That, he concluded, was where the difference lay. He had never before associated going to church with being happy. For him church had always been a very sacred, solemn kind of place, all statues and stained glass windows, faded pictures and formal pews, dark clothes and long faces. As he came to contemplate it further, he began to ask himself, why should they not be happy? If they felt like he had come to feel since the day he handed his life over to God, they had a lot to be happy about!

By the time Wednesday came Billy was beginning to change his mind about Victory Praise, and when Clinton phoned him on Thursday night to ask him if he would like to go with him again on Sunday night he had it changed. Yes. He would go back.

Billy found it much more enjoyable on his second visit, hugging apart. He knew what to expect from the praise and the preaching. They really made him feel closer to God. But he couldn't have the hugging.

When the service was over yet another friendly man came across to speak to the visitor, whom he had been informed was a 'new Christian.' "Hello, Billy, I'm Willis Mc Dowell, the assistant pastor here," he began. "We are pleased to have you with us. As part of my ministry I share the responsibility for visiting the members of our congregation in their homes. Would you mind if I called up to see you at home some day this week?"

Billy thought for a moment before accepting the offer on one very clear condition, "Wait until I tell you," he replied. "You are welcome to come up if you want as long as you promise me one thing. That is that you won't start hugging me!"

"I promise, honestly!" Willis agreed with a smile, and a day for him to 'call up' was arranged.

That visit helped give Billy a massive thrust forward in his Christian life. It helped teach him something about his salvation and it was also to afford him an outlet for his interest.

He sat enthralled as Willis explained to him from the Bible what it was that had actually happened that afternoon in the hospital. It was mind-boggling to Billy. God didn't see him as a sinner any more. His sins had all been dealt with when Jesus died on the cross. As far as God was concerned, Billy Morgan wasn't the old Billy Morgan he used to be. He now saw him as a totally different person, a new creation in Christ Jesus. Billy had, in fact, he was to discover to his delight, been born all over again, spiritually!

Before leaving that afternoon Willis said, "Billy we have a drop-in centre we run in Ballee. All kinds of people from that housing estate call into it and we have activities for all ages. Would you like to come over to Hope House, as we call it, and talk to the young people some time? They would love to hear your story. We are forever telling them that God has the power to change lives like yours and theirs. You would be a living testimony to our witness if you would come."

"That would be great. Of course I'll come!" was Billy's immediate reaction.

He went over the next week and soon became involved in all the activities taking place there. He found the work very fulfilling. After returning from hospital he had been afraid to go out in case he met some of his former cronies. Now, recognising that he was a new person however, he found that a renewed confidence had accompanied his new identity, and he just wanted to serve the God who had made such a difference in his life, amongst the people of his town.

Soon Billy was out at the centre two full days every week, cutting lawns, cleaning windows, delivering second-hand furniture to appreciative pensioners and single parents and driving elderly people to medical appointments. He loved it too! What a joy to be able to demonstrate his Christian faith in such a practical way.

It wasn't long either until he was attending every meeting at Victory Praise. He was learning so much about the love of God, the life of Christ as an example for living, the death of Christ as a provision of salvation and the teachings of the Bible on Christian principles that he couldn't wait to be there. On Sunday mornings he left home at nine o'clock to do the twenty-minute walk to church for the eleven o'clock service. He wanted to be first into the building as soon as the doors were opened. It was the same on Sunday evening and during the week. First man on the doorstep was always Billy Morgan!

Within months of starting to attend Victory Praise Billy realised that he ought to be baptised, and so put his name down on a list to go on a trip to Israel. It all sounded so wonderful. He had the vision of being baptised in the River Jordan at Pentecost. What could be more scriptural than that? he thought.

Billy's idea didn't seem to be God's plan, however. He was very disappointed to find in a matter of weeks that the trip was oversubscribed and he couldn't go.

As an alternative, arrangements were made for Billy to be baptised one Sunday evening in Victory Praise. Realising that he could do in Ballymena what he couldn't do in Bethabara, Billy invited twenty of his former friends to come and witness his baptism. Although only two of them troubled to turn up he was pleased to see them, and unashamed to make before them, and the capacity congregation crammed into the church, a public confession of his faith in Christ.

With his spirits high and his face shining afterwards Billy felt his entire being tingle with spiritual joy as people came across one by one to encourage him. He felt that he had been transported into some kind of ethereal, heavenly realm.

It must have been something extraordinary for three men actually couldn't restrain themselves from hugging him, and Billy didn't even object!

9

WHY DON'T YOU DO SOMETHING ABOUT IT?

BILLY WAS OVERJOYED at all the unfolding thrills of the Christian life. It seemed that he was learning something new about his Saviour and what He meant to all those who trust Him, or enjoying some unexpected blessing from His bountiful hand, or both, nearly every day!

He loved meeting all the people out at Hope House in Ballee and doing what he could for them, but that was only two days a week. Could he not be demonstrating his appreciation to God for all His kindness on the other days as well? Billy was so full of the joy of his salvation that he wanted to be serving the Lord every waking hour.

How could he go about it? Where would he even start? Billy would never aspire to be a pastor or a preacher, and he certainly couldn't imagine himself as a worship leader either. Were there any job opportunities in the realm of Christian ministry for a man like Billy Morgan, converted drinker, drug addict and dealer?

When a lady approached him one afternoon with a proposal that she said would help both himself and others, he was caught unawares. In the mix-up of the moment he made a hasty response which he was very soon to regret.

It happened on the street in Ballymena. Billy met Amanda who worked in the Family and Addicts Support Group in the town. She had known Billy from the days when he was much in need of the advice and aid the Group could offer. When he told her of his conversion, adding that he 'never touched the stuff now,' she saw in him the kind of person for whom she was always on the lookout.

"Why don't you come over to the centre in Mill Street and work as a volunteer?" she suggested. "You would just be the right man for that kind of job. Been there, done that. You would have a lot to offer the people who come to us, and besides, it would be good for you as well."

"Oh no, Amanda, I wouldn't be cut out for that," was Billy's immediate reaction. "I wouldn't know what to do, or say."

"I think you would, Billy," Amanda insisted, "Once you were with them, you would know better than most what to say." No matter how hard she tried to persuade him, though, Billy refused to change his mind.

He wasn't long home until he began to feel bad. Had this been the opportunity he had been looking for to extend his work for God? And he had turned it down flat.

For some reason Billy had this vision of working in a comfortable Christian-type, church-type atmosphere. The idea of becoming a volunteer in an organisation dealing with drug addicts had never crossed his mind.

When he came to think it over in the cool of the evening, in the solitude of his flat, he couldn't come up with one single reason why he **shouldn't** volunteer.

Had Jesus not been called 'the friend' of all kinds of sinners?

Had He not gone out of His way to speak to crooked tax collectors and ostracised, immoral women?

Had he not instructed His followers to 'go into all the world and preach the Gospel' to everybody you meet?

Would 'all the world' not include the Family and Addicts Support Group in Ballymena?

It must, of course!

A week later he met Amanda again. She was possibly not going to mention her suggestion of the previous Saturday, remembering how adamant Billy had been that he 'wouldn't be cut out for that.' He though, wasn't going to let the opportunity pass.

As the week had gone on he had been kicking himself for his stupidity. He had been telling God that he would like to show his love for Him and for others in more and more practical ways, and when someone came along offering him the chance to do just that he had turned it down.

Amanda had only just finished her, "Well, Billy, how are you today?" friendly greeting when he was in with his question.

"Tell me this, Amanda," he began eagerly, like someone conscious that every second was precious, "that idea you put to me last week about working as a volunteer in the Family and Addicts Support Group, does the offer still stand? I was just thinking that although I work for the church out in Ballee two days a week I could go to you the other three. Would that be possible?"

"Of course it would," came the enthusiastic reply. "It's mostly part-time volunteers we have up in Mill Street. When would you like to start? The sooner the better. We are always looking for new staff, especially people with your experience!"

It wasn't long until they were discussing details of when he should call to be shown around his new workplace. Neither wanted to waste any more time and so a day the following week was agreed for Billy to be introduced to the work of the Family and Addicts Support Group.

The first morning he walked into the centre in Ballymena where the group met, Billy was transported back in time. As he looked around at the people sitting there gazing vacantly ahead or ambling aimlessly about, he was struck by the sense of sheer hopelessness that existed amongst them. He found the feeling of futility and silent fear that seemed to pervade the place almost frightening. The scary thing was that up until just about a year before he had been amongst them

His had been one of those vague, expressionless faces.

He had been grinding along in a pointless, purposeless existence.

He knew exactly how it had felt then, but he also knew how he felt now.

And what a mighty change it was!

Billy had so much to tell these people, if only he were to be given the chance.

It took him a week or two to get to know all the 'regulars,' but when he did the opportunities soon presented themselves. As he commenced working closely with them, listening to their stories, encouraging where appropriate and helping where he could, he began to be granted openings to speak of his faith in Christ.

This wasn't surprising. Billy Morgan was a walking, talking visual aid.

Hundreds of people in the town knew him. They remembered what he had once been like, and were amazed at what he was now.

All that was left for Billy to do was tell them what had made the difference.

As weeks of volunteering in the Family and Addicts Support Group rolled on into months, hardly a day went by when the transformation that God had made in Billy's life didn't become the subject of his conversation with somebody.

It was a great pleasure for him to be able to become involved with people like these. So great was his fervour that he soon began to feel that this work he was doing in both daytime centres was just a mere appetiser of what he could yet be doing for God. There must still be much more to be done, and other ways of doing it. There had to be other hurting people somewhere. Where could Billy go to find them?

There had been, around that time, a series of weekends when young people had been fighting and injuring one another, or overdosing on drugs or having too much to drink and being found unconscious or inebriated on the streets of Ballymena. The local newspapers were full of it and it was being reported on radio and TV.

Billy was sitting in his flat reflecting on all that was supposed to be going on around him in the town one Friday night when the thought hit him like a hammer blow. "What's the point of just sitting moaning about what is happening out there? That's not helping anybody. Why don't you do something about it?"

It was a sobering, challenging thought. He was on his own, had no ties to keep him in the house and he knew every pub, club and drinking den in Ballymena. Better than that, he also knew Jesus, and what He could do for anybody who would trust in Him. It dawned on Billy that if he were to go out and show these people something of the compassion of Christ then he might be able to eventually to see them brought to Him.

That wouldn't happen, though, if he were to remain at home complaining about 'the young people of today,' and lamenting that we 'must be living in the last days.'

Why wasn't he doing something about it?

Pulling on his coat he walked straight out into the winter night. It wasn't far from his house to the first club he could think of, and when he reached it he spoke to the doorman.

"I want to give you my phone number," Billy told him. "If you ever find anybody coming out of here in any sort of trouble, I mean if they have been hurt in a fight, or are drunk and vulnerable, or have overdosed and can't get home, anything like that, let me know. I will come and help them."

Although rather surprised that anybody should care enough to be bothered to look after 'irresponsible' young people who had put themselves into a position where they couldn't look after themselves, the doorman agreed that he would. Billy walked on from there to the next club where he left the same message. And to the next, and the next...On his way from club to club he also called from pub to pub, leaving his telephone number, and offering to help anybody in need.

He did the same the next Friday night, and again the following one. He was on his way home that third Friday, wondering if his good intentions were nothing more than just a waste of time, when he heard a young lad shouting.

"Please help me!" he was calling out, obviously in a state of distress. "It's my mate!"

Billy hurried up to where the chap was leaning over another young man, who was 'out of it,' lying in the gutter at the side of the road. "He has overdosed on heroin," the lad told Billy. "What am I going to do?"

He may not have known what to do, but Billy did. He had seen young people in that state die before. An emergency call from his mobile soon had an ambulance on its way to the scene. Billy stayed with the lads until the ambulance arrived, and whisked the fellow who was unconscious off to hospital.

It was for people like him that Billy was out there, and he determined to continue.

There were discouragements as well as gratifying moments in the weeks that followed. Some nights he didn't find anybody to help. One night a drunk girl ridiculed him loudly and publicly for being a Christian. There were times when he was tempted to give it all up, but didn't.

When someone told Billy of the work of a group called Night Light, which was run by a man called John Luke and a team of volunteers on the streets of Belfast every weekend, he decided to go up to the city one Friday night and see it for himself.

He was impressed. Rather than waiting for others to contact them to let them know of a need, the Night Light team set up a table, offering free tea or coffee to anybody who passed by. As the pubs and clubs were releasing their patrons on to the streets many young people would take a cup of coffee and remain to chat. What Billy noticed, and it thrilled him, was the manner in which the team created openings for Christian witness. Conversations, which could have begun about anything from the state of the weather to which team was going to win the Premiership, ended up with the person standing with an empty coffee cup in his or her hand, asking questions about God.

Billy found Night Light inspirational and he wanted to do something similar in his own town at the weekends. He realised, though, that he would need help. It would be impossible to carry on this venture for God, and the young people of Ballymena single-handed. When he approached the leadership of his church, Victory Praise, and told them of his vision, they were most supportive.

If he was expecting others to become involved in this outreach of love and care Billy recognised that he would have to create an organisation with an individual identity. Quite simply, he would have to give it a name.

When he had given the matter some thought, and discussed it with others who had expressed an interest in helping him, it was agreed that they should call the group they were attempting to establish, Club Reach. On the first Saturday night they headed out onto the streets of Ballymena with their table, tea and coffee, there were eight of them. Billy and the seven who had volunteered to help him were greeted with mild surprise at first, but nonetheless it seemed that what they were endeavouring to do was appreciated by one or two of those who stopped with them.

It was confidence-building work at first, but as they talked to young people, and made the Club Reach telephone number available to not only the pubs and clubs but also to taxi-drivers and the police, contacts began to be made.

One of the first of these came on a Friday night in July 2004. Billy had been to Hillsborough Bible Week in the Elim Church in the County Down village with some friends from Victory Praise. He had just arrived into his flat in Ballymena when the phone rang.

"Hello, is that Club Reach?" the man's voice at the other end of the line enquired. "Two girls have collapsed here on the street. Can you help?"

Billy said, "Yes, of course we can! Where are you?"

When the caller had told Billy the location he set out to help. As he didn't have a car at the time he ran the whole way and found the scene just exactly as it had been described to him. Two girls in their late teens or early twenties had collapsed on the street. They were hopelessly drunk. Legless.

From the scene Billy phoned two female volunteers from Club Reach, and outlining the situation briefly, asked them to join him as quickly as possible. They came to the scene as fast as they could and accompanied the drunk girls home in the taxis that Billy had summoned.

While waiting for the helpers and taxis to arrive one of the policemen who had been called to investigate the 'disturbance' spoke to Billy. He was mystified.

"I don't understand," he began. "Why would you want to do all this, for people like these, at this hour of the night?"

"I do it because I love them, and I love them because God loves them," Billy told him. "You may be new to the town, but the older policemen here know me. I used to be like these young people, drunk and on drugs, and in all kinds of trouble. Last year God came into my life and changed it, and now all I want to do is help kids like these. That's why we set up this group called Club Reach."

Early the following week Billy had a phone call from the police station asking him to call round 'some of these days.' Somebody wanted to see him.

Billy had no trouble finding the police station. He had been a regular visitor there in his earlier days but as he made his way to it on Tuesday afternoon he wondered what this was all about. One thing he did know, however, and that was that he wasn't in trouble. Couldn't be, for he hadn't done anything.

On arriving at the station the duty officer showed him into a room and he was soon joined by someone he knew well. It was the Inspector of the Community Police Unit.

"Hello, there," he said, on seeing Billy. "I just can hardly believe this, and I want to check something out. Are you the Billy Morgan that gave us all the trouble years ago? I used to spend nearly half my time chasing you, and you were nearly as often in this station as you were at home. Are you THAT Billy Morgan?"

"Yes," Billy replied with the hint of a smile. "I am that Billy Morgan" and he then proceeded to tell him about the change in his life.

"And what is this Club Reach that you are involved in? Tell me what it is all about," the Inspector went on to urge.

Billy then began to explain his concern for the young people of the town, and the challenge to 'do something about it.'

The Inspector seemed taken aback and totally amazed all at once.

"That's great," was his conclusion on the matter. "We in the Community Police will do what we can to help you. No doubt we will be contacting Club Reach in situations where we feel we could use you. The more groups and agencies that are working together 'to do something about it,' the better."

Billy was walking on air all the way home. Now it was he who was 'hardly able to believe it.' Imagine! Billy Morgan working in cahoots with the Community Police!

This could only be from God, Billy mused.

Was it not God who had started it all?

Had He not decided to put all the pieces in place to 'do something about' a worldful of sinful, rebellious generations in the first place?

10

FAITH, FIRE AND THE WASH BASIN FAMILY

THUS BEGAN A very interesting and fulfilling year for Billy Morgan and Club Reach. He and the team of loyal volunteers established themselves on a regular 'pitch' in Broadway, in the centre of Ballymena, every Friday night. The warmth of summer evenings gave way to the chill of autumn and eventually to the cold of winter and still they were there. The tea, coffee and chance for a chat they were prepared to offer to shivering young people on the street were usually gratefully accepted.

In the late spring of 2005 Billy had a surprise telephone call from a Northern Ireland television company. They were planning a series of programmes about the young people of the province, focusing mainly on what they considered to be the most important issues in life, and why. The feature, which they hoped to call 'The 'I' Generation' would be filmed soon and broadcast, hopefully, 'in a few months time.' It was the producer's intention to include it, as a 'special,' in the early-evening prime-time local News presentation.

The reporter on the line had a few questions to ask about Club Reach. "What is it all about?" she was anxious to know. "Who are these young people who are involved?" and most puzzling of all to her probably was her query, "Why would they want to stay out to midnight and afterwards serving tea and coffee to others who could well afford to buy it themselves if they wanted it, when they could be in their beds? What is the incentive?"

Billy answered the questions as they came, one by one.

It was all about showing practical Christian love and concern to people who would have little or no interest in going to church. About making it clear that there was more to Christianity than preaching and praying. It included caring and sharing as well.

The young people on the team came from a wide spectrum. Some were students, some were teachers, others worked in shops and offices in the town, one or two were still looking for jobs. Although coming from very diverse backgrounds they all turned out with a singular motive. They wanted to manifest the love of Christ in down to-earth fashion to the people of their own peer group in their own town. Their Christianity had to be comprehensible. It was as simple as that.

These responses must have had a positive impact on the caller. They were probably different to the perception of young people she had heard others express. A crowd of louts and scroungers, yobs and 'hoodies,' who spent most of their time swigging beer, fighting about football, surfing the 'Net and talking for ages on mobile phones, was the impression many people had of them. Now here was a man from something called Club Reach telling her about young people who were prepared to turn out all muffled up in the middle of the night to ply rowdy revellers and half-shot teenagers with tea and coffee. And all for the love of Jesus. This must surely be different!

"Would you mind if I came down some night with a camera crew and filmed your work?" she enquired. "We would stay with you all the time you are out, and then compile a programme."

Unwilling to take such a decision himself Billy gave her the cautious answer, "If you give me a short time to talk it over with the other leaders I promise to get back to you as soon as possible."

When Billy contacted Willis Mc Dowell, who shared the responsibility for Club reach and some others, they were all of one mind. Go for it. They saw it as an opportunity to demonstrate, not 'Oh-what-a-good-boy-am-I!' but that the love of Christ fires and inspires people to do unusual, and often unexpected, things.

Billy called back 'as soon as possible' as promised, accepting the proposal of the TV Company, and a suitable Friday night for the camera crews to roll into Ballymena was agreed.

It was a new experience for the Club Reach team to be filmed at work on the street. Some of them were nervous about being interviewed and Billy and Willis were slightly apprehensive about the outcome. What would the reporters think of the concept and value of their weekly vigil? They spent four hours out with the group, speaking to a number of the young volunteers and others who were the grateful beneficiaries of their late night ministrations. How would it come across when edited and broadcast?

There was a sense of eager anticipation tinged with trepidation during the week in September when 'The 'I' Generation' was to be screened as a feature in the early evening news. Billy, Willis and the team watched all the other units in the series, trying to figure out what their programme would turn out like, but it was impossible to tell. They had to wait all week too, as Club Reach was scheduled to 'go out' as the final item in the series, on the Friday night.

They needn't have worried, however. The presentation, which lasted about four minutes, portrayed their work in a very positive light. It showed a group of young men and women who seemed to have discovered a purpose in life, and this involved a commitment to trying to help others.

The broadcast triggered a two-fold constructive reaction. One was amongst the participants, the other from the viewers.

Billy and Willis were pleased to see how the team had been strengthened in their faith and resolve as a result of it, but the effect of the programme was to spread far and wide beyond the bounds of Ballymena. The Club Reach leaders had telephone calls from various parts of the province complimenting them on living out their vision to do something of lasting value with and for young people. Some even asked permission to join them on a Friday night to savour the Club Reach experience. Such genuinely interested groups were always accommodated, and as a result others have been inspired to commence their own on-the-streets late night facilities for young people. One of the first groups of Christians to visit Ballymena and then take up the challenge was from the Co. Down town of Ballynahinch.

During the summer of 2005, when he was busily engaged working as a volunteer two days a week with Victory Praise in Hope House, and the remaining three days with the Family and Addicts Support Group Billy found himself beginning to reflect on his position in relation to employment. He was claiming Incapacity Benefit since he had been deemed unfit to work because of his many physical disabilities.

Yet he was, to all intents and purposes, working five days a week.

His conscience began to trouble him. He was a Christian and wanted to do what was right. Was this right, though? The problem was that the only kind of work Billy wanted to do was helping addicts and generally underprivileged people. He believed that was what God had called him to do.

As he thought the situation through it all became more perplexing. If he were to come off Incapacity Benefit where would he even begin to look for a job that would pay him for doing what was essentially Christian social work?

The only solution, he decided was to commit the matter to God in prayer, seeking for guidance in this intricate issue of Christian ethics.

A possible answer to the situation came when Billy met Barry Weir from the Wash Basin centre in Ahoghill, outside Ballymena. Barry told Billy that Jeff Wright, one of the senior figures in the Wash Basin had a vision for establishing what they were already planning to call a Freedom Centre for addicts in the district. It was hoped that this would be opened some time in the near future.

If only I could get a job in a place that that, Billy thought, wouldn't that just be ideal?

With such considerations very much in his mind Billy headed off for the Abundant Life Leadership Conference in Bradford, England, in the autumn. When there he began to follow the seminars on Christian work in the community with great interest.

The leader at one of the sessions told the story of John Edwards who had an up-and-running ministry amongst addicts in London. Having referred to John's work as an example, and before going on to develop some other aspect of his address, the speaker remarked, "John is with us here today and I'm sure he would be glad to have a word with anyone interested in this kind of work."

Billy had been thrilled to hear John Edward's work described, for it was exactly the kind of ministry he was so keen to spend his time doing, every day of the week. And if John had any ideas of how he could do it, and get paid for it, to allow him to come off Incapacity Benefit, so much the better!

As the congregation were filing out of the hall, talking away to one another as they did so, Billy noticed that a number of people were speaking to a frail man with glasses, just up ahead of him. Could this be the man he was looking for?

Drawing closer he began to catch snatches of the conversations in front and realised that it probably was. Still unsure, and anxious not to cause embarrassment to either the gentleman or himself, Billy approached him with a question.

"Excuse me, but are you John Edwards?" he enquired.

"Yes, I am," came the quiet reply.

Having identified the person he so much wanted to speak to, Billy then introduced himself, and gave John a brief outline of the different facets of his work in Ballymena. As both men recognised that they could benefit from the experience and vision of the other they arranged to meet again at suitable times over the conference period.

When they did this John told Billy how he had once been an alcoholic and was addicted to prescription drugs. He had been so 'down-and-out' that he had lived in 'cardboard city' in London. After conversion he had begun to help addicts from the city of London and farther afield in very much the same way as Billy had been seeking to do in Ballymena.

John went on to tell Billy of an event he was planning, later on in the year. It was a walk of converted drug addicts from four different directions in Ireland to Dublin. When they all reached the city he was arranging to hold a service of praise and witness in St. Mark's Church in the city centre.

His question to Billy was, "Would you be interested in joining us?"

"Of course I would," was Billy's immediate and enthusiastic response.

It was only when he arrived back home that the magnitude of what he had committed himself to dawned on him. He would be joining the group walking from Belfast to Dublin and the two cities were 102 miles apart!

About a month prior to the date arranged for the walk Billy was contacted by a worried mother in Ballymena. She was terribly concerned about his daughter, Kerry, who was, she said, on drugs and had just had a baby. It appeared that she was 'all mixed up' and to make matters worse there was 'a problem' with the baby too. Could Billy go round and see Kerry and try and help and advise her? she wondered.

Billy felt pleased to have been approached and was only too happy to be of what assistance he could. Kerry was the sort of person he wanted to help, as part of his service to God, and when he first called to visit her he found a young woman in her early twenties with not one, but a whole raft of problems.

She was a drug addict and her little baby daughter had been born with a misshapen head. Instead of the back of her head being rounded as is considered 'normal' the little girl's head was completely flat.

Kerry found it reassuring to talk to Billy. She could easily sense that he cared about her, understood her, and would be both willing and able to help her.

One of Billy's first questions to her was, "What do you call the wee baby?"

"She's called Faith," Kerry told him, giving a brief smile down at the little bundle in her arms.

"That's a lovely name," Billy exclaimed. "Why did you call her Faith?"

"I suppose it must be something to do with God," the young mother explained. "I believe somehow that God is looking after me. No matter how many times I mess up He has always spared my life. That's how I came to name her Faith."

During the course of conversation Kerry told Billy about the difficulty with Faith's head. There was, she had discovered, an American company which manufactured a helmet that could be fitted to a baby's head to reshape it as the child grew. There were two big drawbacks about her getting this treatment for Faith, she went on to confide. The first was that it had to be fitted before the child was 18 months old to have any effect, and the second was that it was not available on the NHS but could be bought for £2000.

That was Kerry's dilemma.

She wanted to do the best for little Faith, but she didn't have that kind of money. Even if she did there was always the chance that her heroin-addicted body would demand that she spend it on dope. What was she to do?

Billy said to leave it with him. He would pray about it, make the need known, and see if he could think of a way to help raise the necessary funds.

Having pondered the situation for a day or two Billy came up with a solution.

Sponsorship. Of course! Why had he not thought of it before?

Kerry needed money to buy a helmet for Faith, and he was walking from Belfast to Dublin. Very hastily Billy had some sponsorship forms printed and began to beg everyone he could possibly think of to give him a donation, however small, for this 'extremely good cause.' Gary, another man from the Family and Addicts centre in Ballymena had volunteered to accompany Billy on the walk and secure sponsors also. The cause caught the imagination of all those contacted and funds began to flow in.

Before the walk began kind donors had pledged more than £1300 to the two would-be walkers. More than two-thirds of the money required to purchase Faith's helmet was set to come in. All that remained for them to do now was to walk from Belfast to Dublin.

On Saturday October 8 a reporter from a local radio station joined Billy and Gary at the start of the walk in Belfast. After they had introduced themselves as being from Ballymena, the interviewer asked, "And where is your back up team?"

"Back up team?" Billy sounded puzzled. "We have no back up team. There's just the two of us!"

They hadn't long started on their journey, however, until they realised that a 'back-up team' might have been a good idea.

The going was tough. By the time they reached their overnight stop in Dundalk they were completely exhausted. They just tumbled into bed and slept soundly. There was more walking to be done tomorrow!

It was worth it all, though, when they reached Dublin, later on the following day.

One hundred former addicts from all over the island had converged on St. Mark's Church, and they each released a balloon from the steps in memory of absent friends who hadn't made it. These were the fellow-addicts they had known who had been killed by their addictions.

Inside the large church that Sunday evening Billy and Gary joined the choir of a hundred former addicts to sing their praises to God for a miraculous and lasting deliverance. Moya Brennan sang. Billy found the atmosphere stirring, exciting, inspiring, challenging. And others must have as well, for when an appeal was made at the close of the service twenty addicts who had been in the audience came forward for counselling.

Billy went home from Dublin on a spiritual 'high.' The walk had proved a wonderful blessing to him, and he was soon to learn, a tremendous benefit to Kerry and her baby as well. Arrangements had been made for them to cross to England within a few weeks to have Faith's corrective helmet fitted.

It was during those gradually coming down to earth again, post-walk weeks that Billy was to have the remaining niggling concern of his life settled, in a most satisfactory manner, too.

He met Barry Weir again one morning and he was able to tell Billy that the Wash Basin were intending to expand their staff, especially with this new Freedom Centre for Addicts now at the planning stage. Someone had asked him to find out if Billy would be interested in joining their team.

Interested?! Billy would be delighted! That's what he had been praying for all summer, an opportunity to live out his faith in the community, helping others who were in crying-out need for help, and getting paid for it as well! This would allow him to do what he most wanted to do in all the world without feeling that he was taking money under false pretences.

Only two things stood between him and his dream job. The first was that he had to find out what his position was with the Social Services Benefits Branch, if he would be legally entitled to work, and the other was that he had to be interviewed by Jeff Wright from the Wash Basin.

When he contacted the agencies that dealt with his Incapacity Benefit, Billy was pleased to be informed of a new provision which had just recently been introduced. It was called New Deal for the Disabled, and under the terms of it Billy would be entitled to take up full-time employment, but if he was found that he was unable to work for a sustained period then he could return to Incapacity Benefit.

Billy was quite nervous on the day he went to meet Jeff Wright. He was the man whose desire to do something worthwhile for God in Ahoghill had seen the wash Basin Christian centre established in the village. It wasn't his Wash Basin image that worried Billy initially, though. It was the fact that Jeff was the Chief Executive of a large local manufacturing company that left him somewhat uneasy. How would a converted rascal from the streets of Ballymena get along with somebody like that?

He needn't have worried. It was brilliant.

After Billy had told Jeff a little of his background, about how he had come to know the Lord, and what he was doing now in the various avenues of his voluntary endeavours, Jeff said, "That's great! You are just the kind of man we are looking for here, hi! Somebody with a heart for the people! We want to reach out to everybody in this village for Jesus. That's all that matters at the end of the day!"

As Jeff continued to outline his plans for a Freedom Centre with an earnest, intent enthusiasm, Billy thought, 'I would love to be working alongside this man! He is on fire for God!'

His prayers were answered, and his dreams came true.

In late October Billy was invited to become the latest full-time member of staff in the Wash Basin. That was soon to prove another momentous milestone in his life.

For the first few weeks in his new job Billy began to imagine that God had relocated heaven to the Diamond in Ahoghill.

How all the staff seemed to love one another thrilled him.

How they all seemed to be striving together for the same end, to see people reached with the Gospel and taught the Scriptures, excited him.

What he found most moving of all was the way every single one of them welcomed him as an equal. They accepted him as though he had been part of the set up all his life.

God had placed him in a happy, loving, caring family. The Wash Basin family.

Little did Billy, or any other member of that close-knit community know, however, that all their Christian care, compassion and commitment was soon to be tested to the absolute limit.

11

THROUGH THE LETTER-BOX

THE DREADFUL NEWS was conveyed to Billy in a phone call.

It had just been an ordinary Wednesday evening. Billy had been invited to speak about what God had done in his life at the Bible-teaching meeting in the Wash Basin the next night and was sitting quietly in his flat wondering how best to go about it.

Then it came.

The news was devastating, unthinkable, and almost unimaginable.

Another member of staff rang Billy to tell him that a fourteen-year old girl who had been a regular, and popular member of the 'crowd' at the Wash Basin youth activities had been found dead. The indications were that she had taken her own life.

Billy hurried into the car and drove the five miles out from his home in Ballymena to Ahoghill. It was all he could think of to do. His immediate reaction was to be with the other members of his new, and extremely caring family in the Wash Basin. He knew they would all be devastated. Billy had only known Cheryl for a matter of weeks. Some of them had known her for years.

When he reached the village he found that most of the Wash Basin staff had congregated in Karen's home. Karen was the member of staff who lived closest to the Wash Basin centre. A number of the young people of the village had joined them. It seemed that everyone was in tears.

The leaders from the Wash Basin tried to counsel the young people, some of whom had been Cheryl's best friends. Most of them had never come face to face with the issue of death before and just didn't know how to cope.

Trying to answer their questions was difficult. 'Why did this have to happen to such a lovely girl?' one red-eyed teenager after another kept asking the leaders. It was a question that some of the leaders were tempted to ask themselves, but knew they couldn't.

"Quite honestly, we don't have the answer to that," they kept telling the bewildered enquirers. "Humanly speaking we just cannot understand it, but all we have to say, as Christians, is that God knows best, and the Bible tells us that His ways are 'past finding out.'"

As Billy was leaving to go home shortly after midnight he crossed to Jeff and said, "I suppose tomorrow night will have to be cancelled now after this."

"No, we can't cancel it," was Jeff's considered response. "Tomorrow night will have to go on as usual. The devil will be trying to cause doubt and confusion amongst us at a time like this, Billy. It says in Revelation 12 that 'they defeated him by the blood of the Lamb and the word of their testimony.' That's what we must do."

It was a wise decision. The Wash Basin was packed out the next evening. People just wanted somewhere to go to be together to share their grief, and when Billy began to give his testimony a sense of tranquillity descended on the gathering. He told how his life had been totally transformed from pointlessness to usefulness, when he had transferred allegiance from the kingdom of Satan to the kingdom of God.

Before Jeff began his closing message he welcomed everyone yet again and then remarked, "The fact that you are all here tonight proves that we have defeated the devil and his evil schemes."

The funeral was a trying time for everyone. As many of the Wash Basin staff as possibly could be there attended, tenderly expressing their profound sympathy to the heartbroken family and friends, and assuring them of their continued prayers for the days to come.

During this most testing period Billy found himself carried along on a tide of communal commitment and care. All his colleagues had been deeply affected by the tragic event and their selfless love for people for God was unmistakeable. He was humbled, but at the same time considered himself extremely privileged, to be called of God to work for Him in such an environment.

On taking up full-time employment with the Wash Basin, Billy had to relinquish his voluntary hours in Hope House, Ballee, and The Family and Addicts Support Group. He had so much enjoyed his involvement with these organisations that he was reluctant to leave, but confident that those attending the two centres would be adequately cared for by the other volunteers.

One person worried him, though. That was Kerry.

For some reason, Billy felt a special responsibility for her ever since the walk and the subsequent purchase and fitting of Faith's helmet. Early checks had revealed that the helmet was on course to accomplish its intended objective. That was encouraging.

Kerry's state of health, both physical and mental, was a totally different, and very worrying matter. She had been suffering from bouts of depression and Billy was keeping in constant touch with her, helping her, praying with her and enquiring about Faith's progress.

One Saturday morning in December Billy had jobs to do in town. The first was to pick up Lizzie, who worked in the kitchen at the Wash Basin in Ahoghill, but lived in Ballymena, and take her out to work. He had then intended to come back into Ballymena and put up a set of shelves for an elderly lady. That was the kind of thing he loved to be doing. Always helping somebody.

As he was on his way to pick up Lizzie, Billy had a call on his mobile from Kerry's mum. She sounded anxious. "I have just been on the phone with Kerry there," she said, her voice heavy with concern. "She sounded strange. She didn't seem with it somehow. Would there be any chance that you could go round and check on her sometime, Billy?"

"No problem," Billy replied at once. "I am on my way to collect a woman now to take her out to her work in the Wash Basin and then I will be coming back into town. I will call round with Kerry as soon as I get back into Ballymena."

It sounded like a reasonable proposal and Kerry's mum was entirely satisfied with it. Someone who understood Kerry completely would be calling with her later on that morning. That was enough to set her mind at ease.

Billy's mind was not at ease, though. He had no sooner switched off the phone until an inexplicable urge came into his mind..

"Go now!" it implored. "Go now!"

He was by that time close to Lizzie's house so he went on and collected her. When she was seat-belted in Billy told her of his concern, and of his intention.

"Would you mind if we called round to Kerry's house for a minute or two on our way?" he enquired. "I've just had her mum on the phone there and she is very worried about her. Says Kerry sounded kind of peculiar with her on the phone a bit earlier. Not herself, she thought. I was going to leave you out and then call with her on the way back, but something is telling me that we ought to go round there now. Do you mind?"

"Not at all, for all the minute it will take. Better to call and check that she is O.K." Lizzie replied. There could be no mistaking Billy's obvious concern, and it quickly rubbed off on to her. "Let's get round there."

As they approached the house Billy had an uncanny feeling that something was amiss. There was no sign of life about the place. A strange stillness hung in the air. All the curtains were tightly closed although it was by then mid-morning.

Billy and Lizzie both hurried up to the door and Billy knocked it.

There was no response.

He banged the knocker even louder.

Still no response.

Thinking that if she didn't want to answer the door to a knock she would surely recognise his voice, Billy rattled the knocker once more and called out, "Kerry, it's me! Billy!"

Still no sound of movement from inside.

This was most peculiar. When Kerry knew Billy was at the door she usually had it open within seconds.

Instinctively, and with a sense of panic setting in, Billy bent down, pushed his fingers into the letter-box and peered through the slit he was able to make for himself.

The first two objects to greet his gaze were Kerry's two feet. Pushing forward right against the door in disbelief, and bending down as far as a stiff-rod neck would allow, Billy looked up.

It was then that he saw Kerry's head. It was flopped forward loosely. Her face was blue. Kerry was hanging from the stairs.

Billy grabbed a tight hold of the letter-box. His body had begun to tremble.

In an effort to explain this uncharacteristic behaviour to Lizzie, who had already asked twice, "Can you see anything?" he stammered out, "Kerry is dead. She has hung herself!"

He was staggering backwards, just about to ask, "What should we do?" when his shocked companion took charge.

"Stand back there, Billy!" she ordered.

Lizzie was a big girl, and stepping forward she raised her leg and with one mighty kick, burst the door down.

Billy rushed into the hall, and grabbing Kerry by the dangling legs he lifted her up to take the pressure off her neck.

"A knife, Lizzie. Into the kitchen and find a knife" he said, between gasps. Lizzie hadn't to be told a second time.

She did as instructed, and then dashed up the stairs and cut the rope.

Kerry's skinny body crumpled down over Billy's shoulder, apparently lifeless.

Gently, tenderly, Billy laid her down on the hall floor and puffed a further instruction. "Phone 999 and get an ambulance to come as quickly as they can," he told Lizzie. "I'm going to try mouth to mouth."

He began the resuscitation procedure at once and Lizzie phoned the ambulance. When the lady in the control room heard what had happened she began giving Lizzie instructions, which she relayed to Billy, and he continued as instructed.

To his delight, and in answer to the panic prayer he was uttering for help and the sparing of Kerry's life, virtually subconsciously, Billy felt Kerry's body begin to stir. It was a miracle.

He and Lizzie had just arrived in the nick of time.

Ten minutes later and there would have been no hope.

The ambulance crew took control of the situation when they arrived and soon Kerry had been rushed away to hospital.

Billy left Lizzie out to her work and rang the lady to explain that she would have to do without her shelves for another week. He was on his way up to Antrim Hospital too.

On arriving there and enquiring about Kerry he discovered that she was out of danger and would probably survive.

It had been close.

During the following days when Kerry was recovering Billy was at her bedside every day, encouraging her and telling her she still had so much to live for.

He needed encouragement and consolation himself, too. He couldn't help asking himself all the 'what-if?' questions and working his way through all the 'if-only' scenarios.

Here again Billy found the prayer support and wise counsel of his Wash Basin family invaluable. They were always willing, at any time of the day or night, to listen to him, pray with him or advise him.

What they couldn't do, however, was erase from his mind the vision of his little friend Kerry hanging limp, like a blue-faced rag doll, in her own hall.

The scene through the letter-box was yet another nightmare image to imprint itself forcefully into his memory.

And it will remain there forever.

12

COMING DOWN THE MOUNTAIN

THE BUSTLE OF Christmas Eve, 2005, had gone from Ballymena and a sense of silent waiting had descended on the town when Billy Morgan left home at 11.30 p.m. He was on his way to St. Patrick's Parish Church for the Midnight Communion Service to welcome in Christmas Day.

It was something he had done every Christmas Eve since becoming a Christian. His purpose in going was two-fold. Initially he wanted to celebrate the coming into the world of the Saviour of the world, more than two thousand years ago, but at the same time it afforded him the opportunity to reflect on his recent past.

What happened exactly thirty years before had been a terrible and tragic turning point in his life. The words of the communion service ordered Billy to 'do this in remembrance of Me,' and he did, praising God for preserving and then saving him. He thanked God that he had been forgiven for all the sins of his former life, but then kneeling down in the pew in the old-fashioned and musty, yet expectant and joyous, atmosphere of a traditional church decorated for Christmas, he turned to prayer.

His passionate plea was for the family of the woman who had lost her life in the accident. Billy had no idea where they were at that present moment, but he prayed that they would be comforted, and come to know the real reason why Jesus Christ came into the world more than twenty centuries before. What he had been aware of, though, was that when his thoughts went back to that traumatic Christmas morning in 1975 he was overcome by genuine concern for those whose lives had been devastated by his folly. In recognition of this he re-dedicated himself to the service of the Lord and prayed that in the coming year devastated lives might be touched and helped by his Christian commitment.

When Billy left for home after the service he felt surrounded by a sense of serenity. He was ready to celebrate Christmas, the season of peace and goodwill to all, in a mature and meaningful fashion.

The dawn of the year 2006 found Billy Morgan enjoying every moment of life. He loved working in the Wash Basin, surrounded by people who shared his passion and vision for seeing others contacted with the good news of freedom, life and love in Jesus Christ. Since he now wished to concentrate on this new challenge of care he left the running of Club Reach into the capable hands of Willis and some others.

Something happened in Ballymena one Saturday night in May 2006, however, that was to find Billy being invited to go out again on to the streets with the team. The murder of a fifteen-year-old lad by a gang of others during a period of sectarian trouble in the town had caused a heightening of tension between the two communities.

Shortly after the murder Billy and Willis were invited, as representatives of Club Reach, and as people who had a concern for the young people of Ballymena, regardless of who they were or where they came from, to attend a prayer meeting in the housing estate from which the murdered boy had come. This had been organised by the members of Hillside Community Church in the estate and was to be held outdoors on one of the communal greens. It was planned to give caring Christians the opportunity to show sympathy for the victim's family and pray for them and for reconciliation amongst the opposing factions in the town.

Billy and Willis were happy to attend and at the end of the prayer vigil they had the opportunity to speak to some of the distraught young people who attended. For Billy it was a chance to counsel yet another group who were struggling to come to terms with the reality and finality of death in their immediate experience.

On their way home in the car Willis had two questions for Billy. The first was, "Do you think it will be wise to go out onto the streets as usual, next Friday night, considering how feelings are running in the town at the minute, Billy?"

"Yes. I think Club Reach ought to be out there, showing loving care to anyone on the streets. I think we have just seen there up at that prayer meeting that the young people of the town are in need of counselling and if the Christians aren't able to offer it to them, then who can?" Billy told him.

The second question Willis asked seemed to him to be a natural progression from Billy's response to his initial enquiry. "Would you be willing to come out and stand with us for a few nights, Billy?" he was anxious to know. "I am well aware that you are very busy in the Wash Basin, but it was obvious from the way the young people were talking to you this afternoon that they hold you in high regard. You have an easy and undemanding approach and they appear to feel confident around you. What do you think?"

Little did Willis know that Billy had already been contemplating doing just that, if wanted. His suggestion merely confirmed to him that it was something he ought to be doing and on the following Friday night he was out at Broadway with Club Reach once more.

It was eerie that night. There were very few people on the streets and the big majority of that tiny minority who were out, were hurrying past in silence, obviously wary of saying anything to anybody. In the course of the evening the team were only able to serve tea or coffee to four people, and even then the conversations tended to be both strained and short.

Not to be deterred, Willis, Billy and the group were out the next week, and the next and the next. It took time, but as the weeks went on the Club Reach team were pleased to see more people out and about again on Friday nights. What was even more gratifying was the realisation that the tension was easing. More late-night revellers seemed willing to stop at the table and have a cup of coffee and the atmosphere of camaraderie and banter that had once been a feature of these encounters was gradually returning.

One of the most encouraging conversations that Billy had was with a small group of young men in their late teens four weeks after he had started going out again with Club Reach.

It all began when one of the lads came to the table. Billy recognised that he had been drinking more than was probably good for him and was clearly tipsy.

One of girls had given him a cup of tea and as he was drinking it his mobile phone rang. He answered it and Billy could hear the boy's voice at the other end enquiring loudly, "Where are you?"

"I'm down here at Broadway having a cup of tea," his mate replied. "People are giving it out for free."

"You're having us on!" was the caller's instant reaction to that piece of information.

"No. Honestly, I'm not," his friend assured him. "Come on down."

"Aye. Right. We'll be there in a minute or two!" came the answer and the phone went dead.

They arrived as predicted, 'in a minute or two,' and Billy began chatting to them. They were all quite 'merry' but were willing to listen to Billy when he answered the question one of them asked. It had been put to him before by hundreds of people at various stages over many nights, and was simply, "What are you people doing this for?"

This afforded him the opportunity he needed to witness to his faith in Christ and the desire of everybody in Club Reach that others might come to know Him as well.

The next Sunday Billy heard someone in church speak about the parable of the talents. One man had five talents, another had two and a third had one. These talents, Billy noted, were 'given to each according to his ability.'

As he reflected on this distribution Billy began to wonder if God had given him any talents. He didn't preach and he wasn't a singer, so what abilities had he to use for his Heavenly Master?

For some reason his thoughts went back to Broadway on Friday night. He had enjoyed talking about God to those boys, and they had seemed very much at ease with him. Having mused on that for a while he came to the conclusion that the Wash Basin, Club Reach ,Victory Praise and The Family and Addicts Centre were merely the channels through which he could best use the talents God had given him.

His talents were his experiences.

Billy Morgan had been through so much in life, he could speak to anybody on the street or in a church or centre and relate to them. They could be struggling with drink or drugs, disability or disappointment, long stays in hospital or short stays in police stations, it didn't matter, Billy could identify with them. He had been there, done that. All he wanted to do was use these experiences to help others for the glory of God.

A further challenge to use his talents for the good of others presented itself in June 2006. Billy saw an advertisement in the

'Situations Vacant' page of the local paper. The Family and Addicts Support Group in Ballymena were hoping to appoint a Community Support Worker to oversee the running of the centre in Mill Street. When Billy read the job description his heart missed a beat. It said that the person appointed would be expected to undertake administrative duties in a centre that was working in the community with 'those who have addictions and other related conditions, e.g. depression and self-harm.'

Billy felt in his heart that he ought to apply for this job, but he struggled with the thought of filling up a form and sending it in. He was so happy in the Wash Basin. Everybody appreciated him there and he revelled in the friendship of the other staff and the wide range of activities they were all engaged in for God. In addition to that he had just recently renewed his commitment to Club Reach and it had 'taken off' once more, with new contacts being established on a weekly basis.

Could he leave all that behind to take on the responsibility of looking after the Family and Addicts Support Group? It was a hard choice to make.

He was so undecided about the matter that he waited until the afternoon of the last day before leaving his completed application form into the Addicts centre. When he heard that he was one of twenty applicants for the position, many of whom would have better paper qualifications than he had, he prayed that evening, "Lord if you want me to be in this job then You will have to put me in this job."

In less than a week Billy was informed that he had 'made the shortlist of five' for the position. When he went for the interview, after which the final selection was to be made, one Friday, Billy felt a sense of calm and purpose. He had committed the issue into the hands of the Lord. He would attend the interview and give it 'his best shot,' believing that if God would have him take the position, then he would be appointed to it, against what would appear to be huge odds.

On Monday Billy had a telephone call offering him a position, employed 25 hours per week as co-ordinator of the Family and Addicts Support Group. Immediately after taking the call Billy thanked God for His guidance and began to consider what to do next.

A priority had to be breaking the news of his appointment to Jeff at the Wash Basin. He didn't relish the thought of this because they had all been so good to him, but on the day he met Jeff and Karen, the senior co-ordinator, he found them very understanding.

Jeff spoke for them both when he said, "It has been great having you here Billy and we will be sorry to lose you, but look at the doors this new job will open for you. I'm sure that you will come across dozens of people that you can bring out to the Wash Basin, and certainly to the Freedom Centre when we have it up and running. Let's not look on it as a parting of the ways, but rather as a partnership in the Word. We are all in the business of bringing people to the feet of Jesus."

Billy took up duty in the Family and Addicts Support Group at the beginning of August 2006 and he had been just a little over a week in charge when Ryan called in to see him one afternoon.

It was some time since Billy had seen Ryan. Indeed they hadn't been speaking to one another since Billy had last been a volunteer in the Group and Ryan had been a regular visitor. In those days Ryan had no time for God. His parents, who were sincere Christians, were heartbroken about him. Billy knew this and made occasional attempts to speak to him about spiritual things but he would have none of it. "Don't be giving me any of that stuff. I've had enough of it in my early days to do me the rest of my life!" was a typical retort from him.

This time, though, it was different. Ryan was a subdued character. When Billy saw him so downcast he suggested that they have a cup of coffee together in the little coffee bar in the centre. Ryan agreed to join him and as they talked he shared what had been for him a horrendous experience.

It had happened about six weeks before. Ryan had become involved in a fight and had lost a finger, been stabbed twenty times and had about thirty slashes across his back. Billy had been no stranger to fights like this in his earlier days or to hearing about them as a counsellor who had his 'finger on the pulse' of the Ballymena subculture. He sat and listened intently while Ryan filled him in on all the gory details.

Before finishing his account of the frightful incident Ryan summed it all up with the observation, "You know it was only God who stopped me from being killed that night."

"You're right, Ryan," Billy was happy to assure him. "And I believe that is because God has His hand on your life. You have been surrounded by prayer for years."

They talked on late into the afternoon and when the shaken and scarred young man rose to go eventually, Billy said, "It's great to see you, Ryan. Call again soon, and I will be praying for you in the meantime."

After he had seen him to the door Billy returned to his seat and sat staring at the empty place where Ryan had been sitting just minutes earlier. He had peace in his soul. This was, without doubt, where God intended him to be.

That evening at home Billy reached for the Bible which he always kept beside him and opened it at Matthew chapter eight. He was returning to a passage he had read a night or two before, but which had now hit him with a jolt. It contained a most graphic and concise description of his work, and his world.

The chapter began, Billy discovered, with Jesus 'coming down from the mountain.' It had been wonderful up there. The people He had been teaching were absolutely amazed at both His teaching and the authority with which He put it across. The mountaintop experience could not last forever, however. He had to come down, and one of the first people He met when returning to the bustle of life on the level, was a leper who cried out for cleansing.

It was what happened next in the story that made a big impression on Billy. He read that Jesus 'put out His hand and touched him, saying, 'I will. Be cleansed.'

Jesus 'touched him.' This was unheard of in the culture of the day. It was doing the unbelievable by touching the untouchable. Nobody, but nobody, would ever consider touching a leper. But Jesus did...

'That's it!' Billy thought.

'The Wash Basin and Club Reach have been my mountains. I have scaled mighty peaks in both. Now though, God is telling me to come down from the mountain. He has something special for me to do. He has a few 'lepers' for me to touch.

The people he has called me to work with are people like Ryan, who was beaten up, slashed to bits, 'and left for dead.'

These are the unfortunates that are often looked upon, harshly and wrongly, as the 'lepers of society.'

My contacts could have the smell of alcohol on their breath.

In my 'mission field' the people I am working amongst could have nicotine stains on their fingers.

Many of the young people I talk to will have needle marks in their arms.

The woman that comes into the centre where I work, in desperate need of help, could have a baby in a buggy, a toddler trailing along beside it, and not a man in sight.'

Billy closed his Bible and then his eyes.

"Thank You Lord, for allowing me to touch these people for You," he whispered, his voice breaking. "Help me to do it for Your glory."

PART TWO

The
Paul Winter
Story

13

THE BEST FEELING IN THE WORLD

"HOLD ON THERE a minute. I have something to show you," young Paul Winter whispered to the lad beside him as they were packing up their schoolbags as the end of the science lesson.

The teenage classmate stopped, looked round and replied scornfully, "You. You! What have you got that I would want to see?"

Hesitating for a few more seconds, just to make sure that all the rest of the class had disappeared out through the door of the laboratory, Paul threw back the flap of his bag. A wooden handle stuck out ominously. The thirteen-year old pupil took a firm hold of it and pulled it out into full view.

"What's that?" the somewhat startled observer enquired.

"You know perfectly well what it is," Paul went on to inform him. "It's a hatchet."

"But what I really mean is... what are you doing with it... in school?" was the further stammered reaction.

"That's just the point. What am I doing with it in school?" Paul continued, his voice growing louder, and his attitude more aggressive with every word. By the time he was ready to reveal the reason for the inclusion of such a fierce looking weapon amongst the little-used books in his bag, he had become fiercely dogmatic.

"If there is any more of this carry-on I'm going to bury it in somebody's head!" he announced in a tone that left the boy who had stopped grudgingly to share his secret, completely convinced that he wouldn't think twice about carrying out his threat.

The 'carry-on' that was really making life totally intolerable for Paul was the constant bullying. He had battled through an unhappy, unstable childhood and then an accident when he was just about to start his secondary school education meant that he missed all of what should have been his first year. Having been in and out of hospital for treatment for a full twelve months left him starting Dundonald High School with a group of boys he had never met before.

Paul had found it difficult to make new friends, to break into established gangs. Especially when he was small for his age, having grown more square than tall, not the brightest in the class and easily provoked into unruly outbursts of anger. His lack of imposing physical presence and any ability or even interest in school lessons led to feelings of rejection. Quick to sense even the slightest inkling of an inferiority complex, the bullies had been making his life an absolute nightmare.

Producing the hatchet was the ultimate reaction of a tormented mind in a desperate attempt to end the anguish. This crazy move ought to bring him a result one way or the other, he reckoned. It could prove to his persecutors that he was as tough as they were, without even having to use it, and this would be his preferred outcome. If that didn't work out, though, and he had to 'bury it in somebody's head,' as promised, then the unfortunate somebody could end up dead, but he would have made his point. Paul Winter wasn't the lily-livered useless runt they had taken him for, even though he was spending the rest of his days in custody.

The surprise tactic had the desired effect without the persecuted schoolboy having to resort to drastic action. His expression of intent in the science room spread quickly amongst the school's restless subculture. In the lunch break that same day one of the ringleaders in Paul's persecution came up to him, with a crowd of others at his heels

"I hear you have brought something into school with you," was his bold opening remark. "Have you still got it there?"

"Yes, I have," Paul told him. "It's here. In my bag."

"We don't believe you, do we boys?" their spokesman taunted. "Come on and let us see it."

Without further ado, and realising that this could be a defining moment in his craving for recognition, Paul reached into his bag for the second time that day to pull out the hatchet. It was sharp, shiny and ready for use and left the five or six boys clustered around it not quite sure what to think.

The ringleader summed up the thoughts of them all exactly when he exclaimed, "You're mad! Completely nuts! If they catch you with that in your bag they'll kick you out!"

Paul Winter wouldn't have cared in the slightest if he had been caught and 'kicked out.' He hated school anyway and an expulsion would have increased his acceptance with the anti-everything movement he wanted to break into. It didn't have to come to that, however. The production of the hatchet in the classroom and a corner of the cloakroom had done the trick.

The bullying ceased from that day onward, and what was more the former victim became accepted as 'one of the lads.'

Although Paul was pleased at this, it wasn't a great help to him in either his educational or social advancement. His education went downhill rapidly from that time. He found it much more exciting to play truant and go creating a disturbance somewhere with two or three other, usually older, agitators, than sit bored out of his mind in maths or music classes.

The group with whom he began to associate were already smoking, drinking and sniffing glue on a regular basis. This was their way of achieving the buzz that kept them going.

Paul was very keen to prove to them that anything they could do, he could do. Soon 'Curly' Winter as his new mates had nicknamed him was beginning to go even farther than them in irrational behaviour, just to prove himself a leader among the 'lads.' He was possessed by an overwhelming urge to demonstrate that he could be just that little bit tougher, wilder or madder than the best, or the worst, of them.

One evening he was down in Bangor with a crowd of the lads and they bought and began to smoke some marijuana. Paul wondered what all the fuss was about though, for it didn't do anything for him.

A few months later he went with two older members of the 'gang' to the Isle of Man and when there they bought a big bag of 'grass,' which they started to smoke. This time it had the desired effect on Paul and he began to hallucinate. Curly considered this to be a big step forward. It was his first 'hit.'

For the next couple of turbulent years he continued to demonstrate the aggressive streak that had led to the bringing of the hatchet into school. It seemed that he had a permanent, and very large chip on his shoulder. He was against everybody and everything. No matter where Paul Winter went he ended up in a fight. And if he couldn't find a fight to get into he started one, whether with members of another gang, one of his own cronies or the police who came to sort out the melee he had started. This violent tendency was made worse by the increasing use of drink and drugs and soon every penny he could find was spent to satisfy his growing addictions.

Paul was married for the first time in late teenage. Unfortunately, with his unstable style of life, the marriage lasted for less than a year but a daughter, Leigh, was born out of that relationship.

It was during those roller-coaster days also that Paul ended up in Newtownards Magistrate's Court, charged with disorderly behaviour and assaulting a police officer. When found guilty of these offences he was sentenced to serve six months in Hydebank Young Offenders' Centre.

That evening he was transferred to spend his first night in custody in Belfast's Crumlin Road Prison. Paul found this a dark, eerie place. His sleepless night was punctuated by the defiant shouts of other inmates. They were yelling to each other and screaming abuse at the system. Their latest companion knew he had to make the best of his overnight stop, and the remainder of the six months up ahead. He had chosen to rebel against authority, and authority, to be authority, had no choice but to punish him for his pains.

Next morning the 'young offender' was moved to the Northern Ireland centre for people deemed to be of that description, handcuffed to a prison officer. He was soon to discover that this institution was run with military precision.

On arrival he was made to shave off the moustache he had grown to increase, as he imagined, his macho image. Discipline was strict in his latest abode, orders had to be obeyed instantly and without question and personal and room presentation had always to be perfect.

Within the first week Curly was to learn that this was no holiday camp he had entered. A few mornings after his arrival he was standing outside his room door awaiting room inspection. When the inspecting officer came along he looked the inmate up and down, then peering over his shoulder into the room exclaimed, "What's that I see in there? A Swiss roll?"

He was referring to the bed Paul had made as neatly as he could, an hour before. Taking three steps forward he pulled all the covers off with one almighty yank, issuing as he did so the barked instruction, "Make that bed again! Properly! And I will be back in half-an-hour to check it!"

At the end of his second week Paul met a burly prison officer he had never seen before, on one of the landings.

"Hello, you. Surely you're new. I've never seen you before. What are you in for?" was how he greeted his most recent acquaintance.

"I'm Paul Winter, and I'm in for six months for assaulting 'peelers,'" came the rattled out reply.

"Assaulting peelers!" the officer roared. "Imagine! Assaulting peelers!"

Suddenly the unsuspecting Paul was sent staggering backwards. A strong, clenched fist had caught him, totally by surprise, in the middle of the chest.

"Well there are no peelers in here, mate, but if you fancy assaulting anybody maybe you would like to start with me!" was his accompanying bellowed comment.

Paul acclimatised to these harsh surroundings and learnt how to survive the system, and began to count the weeks to his release.

With most of his sentence served he was being frog-marched across the exercise yard by a Scottish prison officer one day. With a longing look at the big heavy wooden doors that barred his way to freedom, Paul remarked, "It must be the best feeling in the world, just to be walking out through those doors."

"No, I can tell you it isn't," the officer contradicted him. "The best feeling in the world is to know God's salvation."

'God's salvation. What's that?' Paul thought.

'Whatever it is, if it beats getting out of here for a pint and a smoke it must be good.'

14

EXCLUSION ORDER

WHEN HE DID eventually experience what he thought must be the best feeling in the world, walking free out of Hydebank, it didn't bring Paul all the happiness he had imagined. It wasn't long until he was back with his old mates and back to his old ways. Nor was it long until he was back into prison.

During one of his spells in Crumlin Road jail some of the other prisoners told him about a girl who lived in the Sandy Row area of Belfast. "A nice girl, and just your type, Curly," they said. "You ought to look her up when you get out of here."

He did as they had recommended and soon he had moved in to live with the girl. The relationship went well for a while and they had two children, Kerri and Paul.

The only problem with Paul Winter was that he wasn't interested in doing any meaningful work or bringing in any money. All he wanted to do was collect his dole money and 'blow' it with his buddies on booze. He spent his idle days loitering around the pubs and clubs of the Sandy Row and Donegall Road areas of the city, or in the homes of some his cronies, drinking

It was when he was with one of these mates one afternoon that Paul was startled into a realisation of how cheap life had become, and how suddenly death could put a stop to everything.

'The Troubles' were still affecting Northern Ireland and many of the young men that Paul knew were active members of loyalist paramilitary associations. One of them was a lad called John.

That summer afternoon Paul was sitting in the upstairs room of the house of another friend who lived just 200 metres up the road from John. They were listening to some music, and having a drink and a smoke. It was warm, and the sash window was open a little at the top to allow some cool air in and some stale smoke out.

"What's that noise?" Paul asked all of a sudden. He stepped across to turn the music down, and then cocked his head to one side to listen.

"What noise? I hear no noise," his companion replied. "Just turn the music up again and come and sit down. You're hearing things."

Maybe he was right. Paul did as suggested. He turned the volume up again and was just about to sit down, when the noise began a second time.

"What is all that banging?" Paul wanted to know, and ignoring both the music and his mate, he crossed to the window. Pulling the top half down as far as it would go he stuck his head out.

There was a flurry of activity farther down the street.

Turning around to speak in to his friend who had heard 'all the banging' at the second time of asking, he announced, "The police and Army are just arriving at John's house. C'mon, let's go down and see what's happening!"

They bounded down the stairs into the street. Breaking into a run Paul led the way, dodging past others who were edging forward tentatively, obviously unsure of just how far it was safe to go. Women in aprons peered out of doorways. Children had stopped playing and were standing around in little groups watching the police and army vehicles arrive.

As Paul and his companion approached the scene of all the activity the word was being whispered around, "It's young John. He has been shot."

Although the shots had only rung out a matter of moments before the feeling amongst the neighbours who were rapidly appearing out of their houses and converging on the scene had already gelled into a strange mixture of grief and anger. They were full of sympathy for his family but used a series of expletives to colour their description of those who had carried out the killing.

Nothing daunted by the shocked bystanders or bustling security forces Paul pushed right on down to beside John's house. Pressing forward as far as he could he peered over a policeman's shoulder to look up the alleyway he had walked up so many times with John. He would never do that again, though, for there, lying across it, was John's body. It was frighteningly still, and covered with a blanket.

He stood around, dazed, for a while trying to take in the enormity, and finality of it all. From snippets of information he was able to glean from those around Paul learnt that the hit squad had broken into John's house looking for him. Realising what was happening he had jumped out the back window, with the would-be killers firing after him. It was when he had staggered out into the alleyway in a vain bid to escape, that other members of the gang, waiting outside just in case he tried to get away, pumped a few more rounds into him. So Paul had been right. He hadn't just been imagining things. There had been two 'bangings.'

The loss of his friend John made Paul angry. He knew of only two ways to deal with his frantic frustration, however, and neither of these was to prove of any significant help. He just consumed more alcohol, and became even more aggressive towards all those anywhere near him.

His girl friend found this constant confrontational approach and the persistent mood swings that accompanied it, very difficult to cope with, and they split up. The parting was far from amicable and the mother of Paul Winter's two children applied for an exclusion order to keep him away from the house where she was living with them.

One day, just for something to do to fill an empty afternoon, Paul broke the exclusion order and went to the door of his former home. There was nobody in, so he came away again, unable to even raise a row.

With little left to do, and nobody else showing even the slightest interest in either taking him in or befriending him, he walked a few streets further up into The Village area of south Belfast. From there he phoned his parents asking his father to come and pick him up. No matter what happened to him he knew he could always depend on a bed for the night at home.

While waiting at the prearranged spot for his father to arrive across from the other side of the city, Paul was surprised to be picked up earlier than expected. The car that stopped for him wasn't his dad's, though. It was a police car. Some of the eagle-eyed neighbours must have seen him at the door of his former girl friend's house, and aware of the situation, had reported him.

Paul was soon back in court and sentenced to three months in prison for breaking the exclusion order. He didn't really mind that. Prison was an ordered existence, with plenty of company of his own kind.

His sentence was to be served in Magilligan Prison in the northwest of Northern Ireland. Paul was no stranger to this particular institution. He had been there a number of times before and some of the long-term prisoners welcomed him back like a long-lost friend.

After lunch one day the prisoners were sitting chatting in the canteen before returning to their duties. Most of the men around Paul were serving out sentences ranging from five to ten years. A young lad had just arrived a few days earlier, and was 'the new boy on the landing' to the more seasoned inmates.

Anxious to get to know the men with whom he was to spend the next few years of his life, the most recent addition to the Magilligan population enquired, "Is there anybody here called Curly?"

"Who is asking?" Paul replied, knowing that someone had prompted this lad to seek out one of the most notorious prisoners on the circuit.

When he had given Paul a couple of names of former prisoners he had met when serving some of his earlier sentences, he was sure the lad would soon fit in to the prison culture.

"How long are you in for?" the new boy asked.

"I'm doing six," Paul replied.

"You mean six years," the guy went on.

"No way," came the response of the seasoned prisoner. "It's certainly not six years."

"Well it can't be just six months if you are the Curly that the boys out there are telling me about." The questioner appeared puzzled.

"No, it's not six months. You're right there," Paul informed him.

"But you said that you're in for six!" the newcomer repeated, by now totally bamboozled. "And if it's not six years and it's not six months, what is it? Six what?"

"It's six weeks!" the famous Curly told him, to the amusement of all the others sitting about. They had little to laugh about and if one prisoner saw even the slightest opportunity to 'take the mickey out of' another, they did it. And if the person being made to look foolish just happened to be somebody 'green' it was thought to be even funnier.

That particular period in Magilligan seemed to pass very quickly and soon Paul was out again. He had enjoyed his short break 'inside,' for being out created more problems for him than being in. He knew, however, that if his life continued along its usual lines he would probably soon be back amongst his mates once more.

After this latest release nobody in the Sandy Row area wanted to know him so he moved back to live with his parents in east Belfast. They wished above anything else that Paul could get his life straightened out.

Was that possible, though?

Their son was involved in such a cycle of drinking, assaulting policemen and anybody else who afforded him even the slightest provocation, being arrested and sentenced to a prison term, serving it, getting out and starting all over again...

How could he ever earn honest money, or learn to live a normal life?

15

THE USUAL SUSPECT

PAUL'S PARENTS SAW a glimmer of hope begin to flicker on the horizon of their son's dark life when, in 1993, he told them that he had found a job in Lurgan. Although that meant travelling twenty-fives miles from Belfast each way every day, if Paul could settle into gainful employment they would be glad.

He hadn't started work for long, though, until Paul found all the travelling tiresome and rented a top floor flat in the County Armagh town.

The job didn't last. It was impossible to 'burn the candle at both ends.' Paul was working all day and then doing the rounds of the pubs and clubs in the district all night. He was often turning up late, and usually unfit, for work. Something had to go, and it was the job.

This meant that Paul was soon back to his old ways in a new environment and to an even greater extent than before. Out of work meant less ready cash to fund his constant craving for booze. If he wasn't able to make money honestly, however, he had no scruples whatsoever about making it dishonestly. Methods didn't matter but money did. Paul Winter knew, and was soon using, 'every trick in the book' to keep himself, and his habits, generously subsidised.

One evening when out on a drinking spree Paul met a sixteen-year-old girl in a nightclub in Banbridge. They started to chat and when Paul discovered that Stephanie lived with two other girls in a flat just a few floors below him in the same block they began to cultivate a friendship. Paul became a regular visitor in the girls' flat but he was only there to see one resident. He was attracted to Stephanie and she to him and before long she had moved a few floors up in the world and in with Paul in 1995.

This new relationship didn't do anything for Paul's aggressive nature, however, and it came to the stage that he ended up feeling like a prisoner in his own flat. This was because every time he left it he either broke the law in some shape or form, or was accused of breaking the law in some shape or form. No matter what happened in the area, the first man arrested and charged for it was Curly Winter.

Once when an armed robbery had taken place at a jeweller's shop in Lurgan the police arrived up at his door. It was the kind of thing Curly would be up to, and the discovery of a sawn-off shotgun in the drying area of his block of flats proved just too much of a coincidence to ignore. Despite repeated protestations of his innocence Paul was arrested on suspicion of having carried out the robbery but he was cleared of the charge when the case came before the High Court some time later.

Paul was often amused at the state of some of the policemen who came to his door. When 'the usual suspect' arrived out to answer their knock he would find them standing panting on the doorstep, having climbed up all the stairs to the top floor. They would have a charge with them, but were left without sufficient puff to read it out.

"Take your time," Paul would tell them. " I'm not going anywhere. What am I supposed to have done today?"

Although some of the accusations were proved to be without foundation many others were easily substantiated. It was on one of these charges of causing grievous bodily harm with intent to kill that Paul was to be remanded in custody once more.

When in Maghaberry Prison serving out that sentence he had a strange experience one night. He had gone to bed as usual after lockup for there wasn't a lot left to do, and fallen asleep.

During the 'wee small hours' of the morning, and when in a sound slumber he had a very pleasant dream, and that was unusual. Some of the previous dreams he managed to remember anything about until the next morning had been like action shots out of a gangster movie, full of cursing and fighting, knives and guns, crack parties and bottles of booze. This was something completely different.

In his dream Paul had returned to his childhood and the pictures he saw of himself included scenes of serenity that had been largely lacking from that childhood. He was just a little boy of six or seven years of age walking wonderingly through a beautiful garden. The sun was shining and it was pleasantly warm. Flowers of all shapes and shades bloomed in abundance. The only three sounds that he could hear were pleasant. There was a bird singing somewhere, although he couldn't see it, bees buzzed and hummed as they zoomed from flower to flower and a stream that he had already crossed once on a quaint little rustic bridge trickled and babbled and gurgled and sparkled in the sunlight.

As he continued to walk through this idyllic setting he heard a soft voice whisper, "Let me lead you through this beautiful place,"

The little boy in the dream world raised his left hand, as though reaching up to clasp the hand of a loving caring adult, who was walking alongside. Although there was nobody there that he could see, Paul, in his dream, kept walking on, hand held up, as though clutching that of somebody beside him.

Occasionally the voice would come again, soft and low.

"Stay close to me and you will be happy for the rest of your life," it would promise.

"If you come and live with me, then you will have this peace that you feel now in your heart for ever," it assured.

Paul wanted more than anything to remain in that place for as long as possible. It represented, to him, a fantasy realm that he never knew existed. He felt a warm glow of contentment and a sense of total security as he ambled around that garden of his dream. Nothing disturbed the peace there, and nothing threatened his life. Contentment and security were two feelings that he had known very little about as a boy of six or seven.

Now, though, back at that age in his dream, he felt at rest. He was in a land of sweet delight being comforted by an unseen but tangible presence of total peace.

Unfortunately for Paul his dream was of short duration, and when he awoke next morning he was back to earth with a bump. His prison cell was a far cry from the blissful land he had visited in fancy during the night, but he still felt a strange, lingering hard to explain sense that something unusual but he wasn't quite sure what, had occurred. It was as though some supernatural power had chosen to invade his mind and call him to come and follow it.

Could it have been God?

Paul didn't know. He had never had a lot of time for God and heaven and that kind of thing. It was peculiar, but sort of pleasing anyway, whatever it was.

Just about a month before he was released from prison at that particular time Paul had another dream. This was no boyish walk through a beautiful garden, however. Rather it consisted of a man's voice with a clear message. Paul remembered the words for they didn't seem to make any sense to him.

"When you get out of here, if you see Kenny," it declared, "tell him there's much to do and not much time to do it."

Who was Kenny? Paul had met a lot of men in his time, both in and out of prison, but no matter how hard he racked his brain he could not think of anybody called Kenny.

And what was he to do?

In such a hurry too?

Paul then started to worry about himself.

Am I going off my head? he began to wonder.

16

MISSED IT AGAIN!

ONE OF THE few bright moments in a very bleak existence for Paul came in August 1997 when Stephanie and he welcomed baby Ashley into their unstable world. The little one gave them great joy, and for a while, with both new parents united in their desire to do the best they could for her, things went well.

With Paul, though, every attempt to start afresh only lasted a short time. A wild party somewhere and he was apt to slip back into his old ways. No matter how hard he tried to clean up his act, if there was a riot or a robbery anywhere in Lurgan, Paul Winter was usually suspected of being involved in some shape or form. This did little to increase any sense of personal achievement within him or help him foster self-esteem.

There was something that Paul couldn't understand after his latest release from prison and around the time of Ashley's birth. It was an increasing, albeit still fuzzy and faraway, feeling, possibly triggered by the dream about paradise in prison. He was beset by a creeping consciousness that there was a God out there somewhere, who actually cared about him. He had become aware for the first time, and it seemed almost subconsciously, of Bible verses on boards outside churches, and the occasional mention of God in radio and TV programmes. Years ago he would not have paid any attention to such things, but now his mind afforded them at least a nodding recognition.

In the early summer of 1998 Paul and a friend left Belfast on the Stranraer ferry. Paul said he was going to Scotland to 'live it up for a while' but really he knew in his heart that he was running away from something, but he wasn't sure what it was.

Could it be the responsibilities of parenthood?

Or was it something to do with the fact that he was only responsible for half the trouble in Lurgan but blamed for all of it?

Perhaps this sneaking sense of the supernatural had something to do with it.

Paul wasn't sure why he felt such a compulsion to escape from Northern Ireland, nor did he care. He and his friend were 'going to have a blast' in Scotland for a while. Where they ended up wouldn't matter. The important thing was the starting out. To be away anywhere would be better than being at home.

Their plans didn't quite work out the way they had hoped, however. As Paul came down the gangway from the ferry he spotted a police car on the quay. 'Here we go again,' he thought. 'I wonder what I am supposed to have done this time.'

He didn't have long to wait to find out.

A police officer came across and asked him to identify himself. On giving his name Paul was informed that he was being taken to the local police station. When there he was charged under the Prevention of Terrorism Act and remanded in custody. Within days he was brought before the courts and sentenced to three months in prison.

So there was no such thing as escaping, it seemed. His past was always chasing him, and what was worse it was developing a frustrating habit of catching up.

When serving out this latest sentence in Glasgow's Barlinnie Prison, Paul made a telephone call to Stephanie one day. She sounded excited. "I've got something wonderful to tell you, Paul," she began, enthusiastically. "Ashley has started to walk! She took her first steps today!"

It should have been music to daddy's ears. Paul tried in vain to mirror some of the young mother's exuberance as he replied, "That's wonderful, Steph." It sounded flat. The words were right but the frame of mind was wrong. The thought was there but the thrill was missing.

Paul was struggling to sound pleased that Ashley had begun to walk, for he felt the sharp arrow of conscience pierce him right to his innermost being. Why am I such a dead loss? He kept thinking. I'm really not much good to anybody.

He phoned his mother the next day and when she asked Paul if he had any news he replied, "Yes, I have. The child has started to walk. Steph phoned yesterday to say wee Ashley has taken a few steps on her own."

Grandmother hadn't time to get out her intended, 'That's great Paul.' Her son was rattling on to express his rueful reaction on the subject. "There I am," he told her. "I've missed it again!"

Life was obviously going on as usual for the family outside of prison and he was constantly losing out. Yet he never seemed to 'learn his lesson.'

When he had served his sentence and returned to Lurgan, Paul tried to pick up the loose ends of his life again with Stephanie and Ashley. It was hard, though, for he was in a most unsettled state of mind. It was being pulled three ways. There was always the desire to go out and have a wild time, do 'a job,' drink all night or start a fight. This was countered by his growing sense of futility and uselessness. He often thought he would like to live the life of an honest man, a caring father and a decent citizen, but he couldn't. It was just not in his nature.

Added to this there was always the increasing perception that God was after him. It wasn't that the Divine Presence was trying to get at him, or punish him for his wayward behaviour. Rather it seemed that He would like Paul to stop and consider a few proposals He had to put to him, but the criminal father and frequent fighter was in no mood to listen.

In the few months after he arrived home three different sets of people arrived at his door, giving out Gospel tracts, and on one of the occasions he began a conversation with them. These people seemed intent on telling him that he needed a change of life, which was something that he already knew. They asserted, however, that trusting in God was the only way that any sort of an effective change could be made. Before leaving the door they also warned Paul against losing his 'soul.' He wasn't awfully sure what this was, but the people speaking to him seemed completely convinced that it would be quite a disaster to 'lose' it.

After having had the third lot of Christians at the door with their tracts Paul thought that his mother must have been sending them. He knew how anxious she was that her prodigal son would soon 'settle down,' and he thought she was sending these people to his house to 'interest him in religion,' thinking that it might 'do the trick'

It wasn't his mother that was sending them, though, he was to learn, on making a few rather direct enquiries. If it wasn't her, then, who could it be? He could never remember having people come to talk to him about God at the door and give him little booklets that all seemed to be about God and Jesus, in his life before. Now he had three sets of them in three months! Where were they coming from? Who was sending them?

Could it be that God had stepped up the pace in the race to catch up with him?

If that were the case Paul decided to step up the pace to run away.

In January 1999 he and Stephanie split up and he absconded to Scotland once again. His first stop was with a chap he had met in Barlinnie. He went to stay in a guesthouse in Dalry and the word soon spread amongst the gangland underworld that 'Curly from Ireland' was back in Scotland.

When there, Paul overdosed on heroin one night and nearly died. The next afternoon, when he was still both weak and sick, some of his mates came to him, asking if he wanted to join in another session of 'chasing the dragon' with them.

"Definitely not!" he announced most emphatically. "That is me finished with that stuff for good!"

Within weeks Paul had a call from 'a businessman' from Wester Hailes in Edinburgh. He needed a 'minder' and having heard of Curly Winter's reputation was sure he was the man for the job. Paul took it on, but was only able to stay there three months.. His boss was involved in some dodgy deals and with Paul's natural inability to stay out of trouble and the police constantly breathing down his neck he considered that he ought to be on the move once more.

It was to Liverpool this time, to another bunch of former prison associates. Again, though, it didn't last. The police were after him for a series of crimes and he decided at length to come back to Northern Ireland. No matter where he went he was constantly aware that he needed to get right with God and no matter where he ran to, this overpowering conviction never went away.

Assuming that Steph would have established a new life for herself in Lurgan, Paul moved back in with his parents once again. He had long since lost count of the number of times he had returned home to try and make a new start, and failed.

Could he make it this time with both the police and God on his track?

17

WHAT'S A MISSIONARY?

PAUL WAS IN his bedroom at his parents' home in east Belfast one afternoon, whiling away the time listening to some music when his father came to the bottom of the stairs and called up to him, "You might like to come down here and see this news item on the teletext, Paul. Do you know any of these people?"

Something in the tone of his father's voice, which reflected a sense of urgency that was more than mere interest, combined with a certain curiosity in his own mind and the attraction of doing something different, had Paul making his way downstairs at once. When he entered the living room the two-page message on the teletext was just rolling over. He caught the headline, 'Massive Drugs Seizure.'

Perching himself on the edge of a chair he began to read. It would appear that customs officers had intercepted a car containing over half-a-million pounds worth of drugs at Dover docks. This huge consignment was intended for use on the streets of Britain.

When the names of those arrested in connection with the seizure were shown Paul suffered a nasty shock. One of those remanded in custody was a Stephanie Lorraine Calvert. Steph! What was she doing there? What about Ashley? Where was she or who was she with?

As the questions began to flood into his mind Paul sprang into action. Ashley was his daughter, and if Stephanie was going to be 'inside' for a while somebody would have to look after the little one. He needed to find out more, and the only person who was likely to know anything was Stephanie's mother, and she lived in Lurgan.

Less than an hour after seeing the message on the teletext Paul was out at the bus stop. He had to catch a bus into Belfast city centre and then a train out to the County Armagh town.

When he arrived at his destination the picture became clearer. Stephanie's mum was able to inform him that a Probation Officer had already called with her to help her make arrangements to travel across to the south of England to collect Ashley. Recognising that he ought to take some responsibility for the care of his child in this situation Paul decided to move back into the house he had once shared with Steph and their daughter in Burren Close. On being parted from her mum, who was being held in Holloway Prison, little Ashley was brought home by granny to find her dad waiting for her in the house.

This represented a mighty change for both of them. The little three year-old girl had been separated from the mother with whom she had lived up until then. Paul, who had never been in charge of looking after a child in his life, assumed the responsibility of caring for her every need. Although Stephanie's mother helped him out on occasions he was soon to discover that single-parenting could present him with lots of problems.

The most telling of these was that he was no longer a free man. There could be no going out and staying out half the night on drinking binges. Paul compensated for this by having some of his mates round to the house in the evenings when they could drink for as long as they liked after Ashley went to bed.

Paul often longed to be a great father but he was addicted to alcohol, and in his sober moments he was thoroughly ashamed of it. As he watched his little daughter move around the house, chatting away to him in her childish language, he often said to himself, "Have I not made one awful mess of my life? If only I could turn over a new leaf."

He would find it hard to change, however. Not only was he drinking heavily but he had also become dependent on prescription drugs. It was not heroin or cocaine Paul was taking now, but tranquillisers, all kinds, and lots, of them. With all the pressures that were crowding in upon him he was sure that if he didn't have his daily dose he would go 'off his head.'

One day Paul took an epileptic fit and that scared him. Ashley's granny was called upon to look after her once more while her dad recovered. On one of Paul's subsequent medical checkups the doctor shone the light into his eyes, and enquired after a moment or two, "Are you taking any drink or drugs that you shouldn't be?"

"No, indeed I'm not," came the lie in reply.

"Sorry, but you can't fool me," the medical practitioner retorted. "Go away and dry yourself out for a week, and then come back. I will probably be able to see better what's wrong with you then."

This rebuke from the doctor alerted Paul to the precarious state of his health, because of his endless consumption of alcohol. When he came to reflect on the consequences should he persist in his habit until he 'drunk himself to death,' it shocked him back to his senses. With her mum in jail he was the only parent with whom Ashley had any contact. He couldn't possibly let her down.

In addition to the unmistakeably strengthening bond which it was creating between father and daughter, Paul's full-time care of Ashley was set to provide him with a couple of other, perhaps less immediately obvious, benefits. One of these he came to regard as a definite asset, the other a welcome added extra.

The definite asset was that it forced him to re-establish contact with Stephanie, and it wasn't long before he was making the occasional trip across to London to visit her in Holloway. This was good for their growing child as it afforded her a renewed sense of security to feel that she had a present and active mummy and daddy again.

It was when people came to his door, as they seemed to do at least once every month to invite him to attend a church service or Gospel mission somewhere that Paul's responsibility for his daughter became a distinct bonus.

"I'm awful sorry but I'm not really free to go out in the evenings," he would reply to any such invitation, by way of an excuse. "You see I have a little girl in the house here. Her mother is not at home and the child will be in bed and I have nobody to look after her,"

To enterprising and thoughtful church representatives who offered to accommodate him with a baby-sitter his reply was invariably, "Aw no. I'm sorry but that wouldn't work. Her mother is inclined to be very fussy about who keeps her, you understand. Thanks all the same."

On rare occasions, when he had no mates in the house, and felt the need of some adult company to lift his mind, Paul would actually invite some of these people in. This happened one afternoon when a man came to his door selling Christian books.

The man seemed friendly enough, and as long as Paul had the excuse for not having to go out to any religious services, he would be O.K. It could surely be no harm to have a look at some of the 'colouring-in-books,' which he had 'in his bag' and which, he claimed, would be 'great for the little girl.'

Having settled himself on the living-room settee the colporteur produced a range of Bible colouring books. He showed these to Paul and Ashley, who seemed fascinated to discover on one of the pages a picture of a young man surrounded by eight rather fierce looking lions. The book-man was able to tell her that the man, who he said was called Daniel, was able to look so cool and calm in the middle of all those lions because 'God had shut the lions mouths, so they could not harm him.'

Paul agreed to purchase a few books and Ashley began to leaf through one of them on a mat on the floor. She appeared to be studying the pictures intently. Glancing down at her, and then across at her dad, the colporteur remarked, "I can just imagine that wee girl growing up to be a missionary."

There was a moment's silence before Paul reacted to that observation, and when he did his response came in the form of a question, "A missionary. What's that?" he enquired, with a look of vague bewilderment. He had a hazy recollection of having heard the word before, and was certain that it must have some kind of 'religious' significance, but wasn't sure what it meant.

"A missionary is a man or woman who leaves this country to go to some foreign country to tell people about Jesus and the Gospel message," the Christian door-to-door salesman was able to inform him straight away.

"Oh, you mean somebody like David Livingstone?" Paul replied, suddenly remembering the name of the one person he had heard about at some stage in his turbulent earlier days that might just fit that description.

"Exactly," the bookseller smiled before going on. "David Livingstone was one of many who devoted their lives to spreading the Christian Gospel around the world. Those people were, and many still are, missionaries."

Having written Paul out a receipt for the books he had bought, the man handed it to him with the observation, "It's been a pleasure to have spent some time with you and your little girl. I believe God has a plan for your life. And hers too."

When the colporteur left Paul hadn't much time to reflect on his predictions about God, and the Divine schedule for his life. He had other more imminent plans to make.

Stephanie's trial on drug-running charges was to be held the following week in Canterbury Crown Court and he was hoping to be there. At that time he was just in the process of arranging to stay over a couple of nights with a former drinking mate from Belfast, in his flat in south London.

The day of the trial came and Paul and his friend arrived at the court to observe the trial and hear the verdict. Paul was no stranger to courts, having been often in the dock. That day, though, he was merely an observer. Stephanie was the one on trial.

When the case was heard Stephanie was acquitted of all charges and released. What a relief!

The couple emerged from the court, and raised the hands they were holding together into the air in a gesture of shared delight. Stephanie stood on the steps, free again. She could scarcely believe it. The next day she would be going back to Lurgan, with Paul, to be reunited as a threesome with the three-year old daughter whom they both loved dearly.

Could they make it this time?

18

CLAP YOUR HANDS AND LOOK HAPPY!

SHORTLY AFTER PAUL, Steph and Ashley came together again under the same roof they all changed to live under a different roof. They moved house as a family from Burren Close to Trasna Way in Lurgan.

It was one evening in early October 2001 when someone knocked at the front door of their new home. Paul went out into the hallway but was in no hurry to open the door. With his background, and so many people constantly after him, from the police to the paramilitaries, Paul was always wary of unexpected callers. Indeed he was so conscious of his vulnerability that one of the first 'improvements' Steph and he had made to their new home was to have a strong metal gate fitted behind the front door. This meant that if any determined but unwanted 'visitors' should manage to break the door down they still couldn't gain entrance to the house.

Before opening either door or gate to anybody Paul checked the identity of the caller by peeping out the little window at the side of the door. Seeing the outline of a man whom he didn't recognise standing on the step that October evening, Paul called out through the door, "Who is it?"

"Hello, how are you?" came the friendly, and patently non-threatening response from outside. "I'm from one of the local churches and I was wondering if I could speak to you for a minute of two."

"O.K. hold on a tick," Paul replied, and with a sliding of bolts and a turning of keys presented himself on the doorstep.

The man outside had waited for the man inside to appear, and when he did the caller resumed the conversation from where he had left off.

"My name is Kenny Emerson, and I am doing a survey about churches and church attendance," the man went on, by way of introducing himself and his reason for calling at the door. "You wouldn't mind answering a question or two for me, would you? It won't take very long."

"No, not at all," Paul volunteered readily. He knew instinctively that this man was genuine and would be easy to talk to, and he had certain views on churches that he wouldn't mind sharing with somebody from a church. He had often expressed them to the boys in a pub but it wasn't often you got the chance to eyeball a churchy type and tell him what you thought.

On top of all that, though, and for some reason Paul was at a loss to understand, something was stirring in his mind, like a lazy lion, yawning and stretching and dragging itself across the boundary from inactivity to action.

Having spoken about the number of different churches in Lurgan, and explaining that he was from Emmanuel Fellowship in Union Street, Kenny went on to ask the first of the questions on his sheet. It was, "What do you think the churches could do to make the most meaningful contact with the people of today?"

Paul had no hesitation in answering that one.

"Just what you are doing now," was his immediate response. "Going out and meeting them in the streets and at their doors. I haven't been to a church for years but I don't mind talking to a guy like you at my house."

There were a few more questions that Paul answered as fully as he could before Kenny went on to ask one that made him think a bit. "You say that you haven't been to a church for years," he began, "so I suppose you may not have much of an idea about what different churches believe or how they conduct their services. I want you, though, to imagine that you were thinking of going to a church. What kind of a church would you like to be in?"

Curly Winter's early recollections of church were not particularly pleasant. He had only gone very occasionally, and usually very reluctantly, as a child with his mother who was a Christian and prayed endlessly for him, to Ballybeen Mission Hall in his home village. His memories of those days all seemed to be negative. Hard seats, formal, well-dressed adults, long and occasionally loud, sermons, and boring hymns with weird words in them. That was the concept of church he had grown up with.

Latterly, however, and especially when he had had been confined to the house a lot during the day minding Ashley, he had spent a lot of time watching the TV. And the set blared away all day, even when he wasn't watching it. Paul pressed the ON button at breakfast time and the OFF button at bedtime, thinking that 'the kid's programmes' would keep Ashley amused.

It was during those days of entertainment and education by television that Paul discovered the God Channel and he would watch an occasional programme on it now and then 'if there was nothing better on.' What attracted him to some of the programmes he tuned in to, often quite by accident, was that the participants actually seemed to be enjoying themselves. The way in which they portrayed Christianity was different from how he had always visualised it.

Although he had never been to one of these gatherings Paul reckoned that they must exist somewhere, and so gave his considered reply.

"What kind of a church would I like to go to?" he repeated the question before coming out with the answer. "I'll tell you what kind of a church I would like to go to. I would like to go to one of those places where they clap their hands and look happy!"

This response obviously pleased Kenny for he smiled broadly as he wrote something down on his sheet. "You ought to come over and see us at Emmanuel some of these days," he suggested. "That is just exactly the type of church we would like to think we are."

"I might just do that," Paul said, as the man at the door was turning to go, without really having even the slightest intention of 'doing that.' Then he added, "You could come back and see me sometime."

"I might just do that," was Kenny's instant reaction. He meant it, though. He had every intention of doing it.

After the interviewer had gone on to ask the next-door neighbour some questions, Paul went inside, closed the door and bolted the gate. There was something about the man who had just left that fascinated him. It wasn't, either, just the fact that he told him there was, apparently, such a thing as a church where people clapped their hands and looked happy. There was more to it than that.

Paul turned the matter over in his mind all day, but it was only when he was preparing to go to bed at nearly midnight that it dawned on him.

Of course! Kenny! It was the name!

He remembered his dream in Maghaberry, and the clear instruction of the vision. 'When you get out of here, if you see Kenny, tell him there is much to do and not much time to do it.'

He was out of prison and now he had seen Kenny, but he hadn't 'told him' anything. Perhaps he would call at the house again sometime, or maybe even, and it was no more than a slim possibility, that he would respond to Kenny's invitation and go over to this 'happy' church of his to meet him someday.

The following Sunday evening Curly and one of his drinking pals, 'Wee Rab,' were standing at a street corner in Lurgan. A chill wind seemed to catch them wherever they stood. Rab had a bottle of wine.

"Here Curly, do you want another slug of this?" He held the bottle across to his friend, but he declined.

"No, not at the minute, Rab," he replied, before pausing to go on thoughtfully, "but I was thinking... I mean... I was wondering... Have you ever been to church?"

"Church," Rab repeated. "Church? I haven't been to church for years. Why are you asking me that, Curly? Are you turnin' good-livin' or what?"

"No, I'm not Rab," Paul assured him. "But there was a man at my door last week and he was telling me about a church called...Emmanuel, I think it is. I told him I might go over to see what it was like. I was thinking we could go tonight."

"Me, go to church!" Rab hooted. "Nobody would want to see me at church!"

"According to this man anybody can go to their church," was Paul's response to that retort. The truth was that he couldn't understand what was happening in his own mind. He had never been a great fan of church all his life, but now he felt this strange urge to go.

"All right, c'mon, let's go," said wee Rab, and Paul and he set off for Emmanuel.

The service had begun when they pushed open the door in their drink-spotted-and-scented overcoats and with tight-fitting woollen hats pulled down almost to their eyes. Somebody in the porch made them welcome and opened the door to show them into where the main service was going on.

The two latest additions to the congregation sat down on a seat half-way up the church on the right hand side. The man at the front was just in the middle of making announcements. One of these was to say that there would be a baptism the next Sunday.

"A baptism? What's that?" wee Rab said out loud. Then turning to his mate he went on, "You'd better look out, Curly. That could be you if you don't watch yourself!"

Paul sensed that there was indeed something 'different' about this church. Even though he hadn't heard them sing, he felt that the people around him were happy. They looked relaxed, and extremely interested in all that was going on.

As the service went on, Rab became more restless, laughing out occasionally. Paul had wanted to come into the church, and now it was he who wanted to get out. There was something about the atmosphere that was making him feel uncomfortable. It was as if everyone in there except Rab had something he didn't, but he didn't know how to get it. To add to the confusion, he realised that even if he did know how to get it, he couldn't be quite certain that he would actually want it.

This sense of unease was merely the minor motive for wanting to make his escape, however. The main reason that he was aware that every time he and Rab engaged in a loud, discourteous exchange, heads were being turned in their direction.

Having prayed that 'the Holy Spirit would lead some of those who had been contacted during the door-to-door visitation programme in the past week, along to the meeting,' at least some in the congregation were beginning to wonder if there hadn't been some kind of a mix up. Could these two well-known alcoholics and trouble-makers, one of whom had an almost empty wine bottle in his pocket, be an answer to their prayers? They had arrived into the middle of their meeting, clearly under the influence of alcohol, and had obviously no idea how to 'show respect in the house of God.'

Realising that those around were finding their presence distracting, Paul said to his pal, "Right, Rab. I think it's about time we were getting out of here." Then half-yanking him to his feet, he shoved him forward, and the two mates stumbled noisily out into the porch.

There were three men out there, and one of them was Kenny Emerson, the person who had called at Paul's door in the middle of the previous week. Recognising him through an alcohol-induced blur, Paul called out, "Aren't you the man that came to my door last week? I have some questions for you."

"I am," Kenny Emerson replied, "And I will be round again some of these days to see you, and hopefully answer your questions."

With that Paul and 'wee Rab' lurched out on to Union Street.

True to his word Kenny arrived around to Paul's house later on in the week and this time he was invited in.

They hadn't been chatting long until Kenny asked, "What is it that you would like to know, Paul? What can I help you with?"

Curly Winter, the man who was known in Lurgan as a drunkard and a fighter, a 'tough wee nut that you didn't mess about with,' was now challenged to express the question that had been on his mind since Kenny had called last week. It had come to him then, and since Sunday night's rather rowdy brush with church he hadn't been able to shake it off, no matter what he did.

He cleared his throat, and then took a quick glance around, as though to check that neither Rab nor any of his mates were listening before saying, "I think my main question is, how can I really know God? I believe that there is a God, but you people down at that church seem to know him in a close, kind of personal way. How does that happen?"

That was just the kind of enquiry that Kenny Emerson liked to hear and he began to explain the Gospel to Paul. He was a sinner, and he probably wouldn't dispute that. There was hope though, because that was why Jesus Christ had come into the world. It was to take the punishment that God in His purity would have to mete out for those sins, so that the sinner would be acquitted from the sentence of sin. God did this because He loved men and women and boys and girls, and wanted them to be fit to dwell with Him, in the home he had prepared for them, called heaven, forever. All people had to do was come to Him, and believe in Him, and he would make them His children.

To Paul it seemed almost too good to be true. It all sounded so powerful and complex, and yet in a sense so very simple, that he found it confusing. He, Paul Winter, with all his sins forgiven and seen as a child of God. It would take a lot of believing, that one.

Before he left, Kenny requested permission to pray, and when he did one of the phrases he used stuck in Paul's mind for days. In the course of his prayer he asked God to 'send His angels to put a hedge around Paul's house and family that they might be protected from harm and danger every day.'

Paul was impressed. This statement lived with him. When he came to reflect on it he began to appreciate that this was already happening. The hedge had been planted years ago.

Come to think of it, for instance, why had he not died, all those times he had been nearly killed in fights?

Or why had Stephanie not been given a long prison sentence?

Or why had they been brought together again with Ashley, the light of their lives?

Was there some purpose in it all?

19

'CURLY' WINTER IS DEAD!

WEE RAB WASN'T all that keen to go back to church at Emmanuel. Once had really been enough for him.

That wasn't the case with Paul, though.

He started missing the occasional Sunday-evening street-corner boozing session so that he could slink off to church.

Stephanie didn't know where he was, Rab didn't know where he was, and he couldn't understand what it was that was compelling him to go. Nonetheless, some supernatural influence saw him stumbling and swaying down Union Street to the Sunday evening service. He had found that a drink or two in the afternoon gave him the courage to make it down there, and dulled the fear of being found out and ridiculed ruthlessly by his mates for having anything to do with 'religion.'

It was the last Sunday night of the year, 30 December 2001. Paul had been to the service and on his way out he said to his

Emmanuel contact, Kenny, "I want to get saved." He had to concentrate hard to get the words out. His speech was slow and slurred.

Kenneth Emerson was wise. He recognised that although Paul could not actually have been described as being drunk, he had certainly imbibed enough alcohol to dull his senses. Being saved involved a momentous decision, an important personal choice, and in his estimation Paul was in no fit state, either mentally or emotionally, to take such a vital step.

"That's great news, Paul," he replied. " Could you come back here on Wednesday morning at ten o'clock? You should be well sobered up by then, and able to understand all that we are telling you about being saved. My brother Philip, who was preaching tonight and is the pastor here, and I will be here at that time. We will both be glad to see you and speak to you then."

Paul agreed to do so, and on Wednesday morning, 2 January 2002, at ten o'clock he turned up outside Emmanuel Church in Union Street, Lurgan. Philip and Kenneth had just arrived a few minutes ahead of him and were in the process of opening the doors to face the challenges of a new year in the service of God, when who should arrive into the foyer right on their heels but one of the most notorious troublemakers in the town.

And he wanted to be saved!

The two brothers both welcomed Paul with warm smiles and one of them went to make them all a cup of tea. When this came the three of them sat down around a large low square white table and began to talk.

Kenneth recalled how they had met and how glad he was that Paul had begun to come along to the meetings in Emmanuel. Everybody had been delighted to see him he said, and since that very first night when he and wee Rab had burst in and caused the rumpus they had both been prayed for regularly in all the prayer meetings. The fact that Paul had come to see them that morning wanting to be saved, was, he claimed, an answer to prayer and 'the work of' something or somebody called 'The Holy Spirit.'

Paul couldn't quite understand some of that but when Philip opened his Bible and began to explain the way of salvation to him, he did understand. It was the same as Kenny had told him in the house, five or six weeks before.

He was a sinner, but God loved him and gave His Son Jesus to bear the punishment that was due to Paul's sin on the cross of Calvary. All he had to do was believe that this was for him, and ask Jesus to come into his life and be his Saviour. It was that simple. Jesus had done all that was required, but it was left to Paul to accept that it was for him.

As Philip was explaining God's plan for salvation to him Paul was conscious of a tremendous burden of sin bearing down on his shoulders. He had been involved in all kinds of criminal activities and had served many jail sentences. Could all this be forgiven? he wondered.

With the Bible open on his knee Philip was going on talking. Paul stopped him and said, "I would like to be saved now."

This was exactly what Philip and Kenneth had been waiting and praying for. Recognising the earnest nature of this declaration Philip suggested that Paul should pray what he described as 'the sinner's prayer.'

Paul was glad to do this. With breaking voice and stumbling words he confessed that he was a sinner with a dark past behind him, and humbly begged God to forgive him. As he did, Paul felt the burden of sin break up and disappear. It was like a picture of a house he had seen once on the News, caught in the grip of a hurricane. The slates on the roof had become dislodged and began to fly away one by one and vanish into the distance.

Having confessed that he was a sinner and fit only to be punished, he then thanked God for His love in sending His Son,

Jesus, into the world to die on the cross for him. Finally, Paul asked Jesus into his heart to be his Saviour and prayed that He would help him in the days ahead and for the rest of his life.

As soon as Paul had finished making that heartfelt commitment to Christ the pastor prayed, thanking God that 'the angels were rejoicing in heaven. He also asked for all kinds of blessings to surround this new Christian.

A wonderful sense of peace flooded over Paul's heart during Philip's prayer. When it had been concluded with a most grateful 'Amen,' the new convert opened his eyes, stood up and looked around. He thought that he was looking out of different eyes. The ordinary everyday things didn't seem the same somehow.

There was a freedom about his body and mind that he couldn't quite understand either. The burden had gone completely from his shoulders. It had been blown into oblivion. He had been chained by it for years without having known it.

Now he was free of it, and he knew it!

Before he left for home, Kenneth and Philip, who both seemed nearly as thrilled as he was, welcomed Paul into 'the family of God.' There could be no mistaking how they felt about Paul's decision for Christ, either. The tears welling up in their eyes represented a true indication of the love of God welling up in their hearts for him, as they did so.

This made Paul feel special. The joy of the Lord had begun to overwhelm him and when he was given a 'new believer's pack,' consisting of a Bible, a set of Daily Readings and a list of all that was being planned in Emmanuel for the next month, he was delighted. He was like a child with a 'lucky bag.' This latest 'new believer' could hardly wait to dive into it to explore its contents. Could it add even more to his happiness?

When he left his two satisfied spiritual counsellors at the church Paul hurried home as fast as he could. The first thing that he wanted to do was tell Steph his good news. He felt so great that he was sure everybody would really want to join in his joy. Philip and Kenneth certainly had back at the church. Surely Steph would, too.

She didn't, though.

Steph had heard Paul promise so many times to reform, to turn over a new leaf, to drink less and spend more time with Ashley and her that she wasn't going to be conned by a sudden outburst of religious euphoria.

"I want to tell you what has happened to me, Steph," Paul exclaimed as soon as he entered the house. "I was up at that church in Union Street there, and I have got saved!"

"Oh," said Steph, without lifting her head from what she was doing. "And what does that mean?"

"That means I have given my life to Jesus. I am a new man. I have been born again!" Paul enthused, excitedly.

"It will be interesting to see what difference that makes," came the flat response. "I have heard all this stuff about reforming and so on before. Give you a fortnight or maybe three weeks and you will be back to your old ways!"

"I won't. I have been changed. Believe me! You'll see!" Paul insisted.

"I agree with you. We'll see," Steph conceded, still unconvinced.

She did see, too. After the first week had passed, and then the second she began to think that perhaps something significant had happened to Paul. He wasn't going out on drinking binges any more but instead he seemed to have developed an insatiable desire for going to church. Sundays or in the middle of the week it didn't matter, if there was a meeting on in Emmanuel Church Paul was one of the first at it.

He was upstairs one evening in mid-February and heard Steph talking about him to one of her friends in the room below. "It's wild!" she was saying. "He's up to two or three in the morning reading the Bible and some wee book they gave him up at that church. And he has started praying out loud too. You can hear him all over the house!"

There was a pause for a minute and Paul thought that was the end of it but then he heard her continue, "I must admit that it's better than having a crowd of those cronies in for a booze-up. At least he is not wrecking the place. And he is a lot nicer to me and the child."

Ashley, 'the child,' seemed to appreciate that something notable had happened in their household as well and she said something that was a great encouragement to her dad one evening. She had been out at a Children's Club in the local Free Presbyterian Church and was sitting on the sofa, legs tucked in below her, watching television.

As Paul passed behind her she said, "Daddy, God is good."

It was quite a profound statement for a four-year-old so her dad decided to quiz her on it. "What do you mean, pet, when you say 'God is good?'"

His little daughter turned around, and pointing down to her chest she replied, "He's good for your heart, daddy."

"You're right, Ashley. He sure is! It's me knows that!" was her dad's instant and emphatic reaction.

Paul had only been a Christian for just over two months and was still rejoicing in his newly-found faith when he learnt something he had never even thought about before, and which he considered mind-boggling.

He was driving up Union Street and was just about to pass a woman on the footpath when a sense of compassion prompted him to stop. The lady was elderly and laden. She had a number of bulging plastic shopping bags in each hand and was making very slow progress. Pulling up beside her Paul leaned across and called out the car window, "Would you like a lift, dear? Those bags look very heavy."

"Indeed I would, son," she replied thankfully. "I'm done. I have been praying all the way from Tesco's that somebody would offer me a lift."

When Paul had seen the lady and her bags all safely into his car they set off towards her house which was still some distance away. As they were going the lady said, "You know I am a Christian and pray to God when I need help. It was Him who sent you to me I believe. You are an answer to my prayers."

Paul told her that he had 'just become a Christian a couple of months ago' and the mature and new believers rejoiced together. It was after he had accompanied her home and was driving off again that the full impact of the exhausted elderly lady's earlier statement struck him.

God, according to her, had actually sent him to the aid of one of his struggling children, who was none other than one of his older sisters in the family of faith. And if God had used him to help her could He not also use him to help somebody else?

It was a totally new concept. Paul had never before considered himself as a servant of God or a tool in the hands of the Master.

He was forced to now, though.

As he continued to attend every possible service in Emmanuel and read his Bible daily Paul became convinced that he ought to be baptised by immersion. He mentioned this to Stephen Glenn, the assistant pastor at the Church after a service and his advice was, "If you are thinking about baptism, Paul, go home and read Romans six."

Paul did as Stephen had suggested and became totally convinced that baptism was a command of God for the believer, and a command he ought to obey. He told the pastor that he wanted to be baptised and was invited to join a series of classes the church had started, to explain from the Bible the significance of this ordinance.

There were, he discovered, seven others who also wished to be baptised and a date was set for a baptismal service to take place. Everyone agreed that since it was a public witness of an inner faith it ought to be held in a public place, if possible. What more public location could anyone think of than in the waters of Lough Neagh at Ardmore on Easter Sunday, Resurrection Day, 31 March 2002?

A large crowd had gathered on the shore that afternoon and they gave a resounding cheer as Paul Winter waded out into the water to be baptised. They recognised it as a twenty-first century miracle. What they were witnessing was one of the wildest men in Lurgan, someone who had been the terror of the town and a pain to the police for years, openly identifying himself with the death, burial and resurrection of his Saviour and Lord..

After Paul had been baptised and as he walked towards the shore he raised both hands in the air in triumphant joy and exclaimed, "Curly Winter is dead!

He is lying at the bottom of Lough Neagh!

Meet Paul Winter everybody!

New man in Jesus Christ!"

20

THE MYSTERY OF THE MISSING POLICEMAN

PAUL WAS NOW on fire for Christ. All he wanted to do was serve others in His name, and tell everybody he met about the mighty change that trusting in Jesus had brought into his life, and the joy and peace he was enjoying as a Christian.

The little lady with the shopping bags had described him as an answer to her prayers. Now he just wanted to be the answer to everybody's prayers!

What seemed like a golden opportunity to reach out to others came on Sunday April 21 when Pastor Philip invited him to come along and share his life story at a meeting. The pastor of a church in New Mossley, on the outskirts of Belfast had invited Philip to be his guest speaker at the evening service and he in turn had recognised this as an opportunity to introduce Paul to giving his testimony in a different environment.

It was a family occasion. Philip was accompanied by his wife Jill, Paul had brought Steph along with him, and Paul's mum, who could barely believe that her son was actually going to be speaking at a meeting, also turned up with a friend and Gail, her daughter.

There was a warm, happy atmosphere as Paul and Steph entered the church. Paul left Steph with his mum and sister and joined Philip and Jill at the front. The background music was setting the tone and Bible verses alternated with church announcements on the screens at the front.

What Paul found hard to understand, though, was that when they came to sing the hymns and engage in a time of 'praise and worship' in the early part of the service there were no words projected on to the screens. He had been used having the words in front of him at Emmanuel. It didn't matter so much to him now because he had come to know most of the words of most of the 'worship songs' off by heart but his thoughts turned immediately to Steph. How would she feel, not knowing what was going on?

When the singing was over Philip introduced Paul and he told, with great enthusiasm and genuine joy, what God had done in his life. It was the tale of an amazing transformation and the congregation were captivated by it. Philip found it easy to present the Gospel message in the atmosphere created by the wonder of Paul's testimony, and as he was greeting people going out later on, Steph approached him.

She waited until most had left and since they would all be going home together she knew Philip would not be going away. Although Paul hadn't realised it, the change that had taken place in his life had made a tremendous impact on her. She had never believed it possible. She had given him two, or maybe three, weeks. Here he was now almost four months on, still rejoicing in his Christianity, and nobody knew more than her that every word he said about being a new creation was correct. He wasn't drinking, or smoking or swearing any more. All that seemed to have vanished completely. And his attitudes had changed too, whether to the use of money, or contact with other people, or caring for Ashley and her. It was nothing less than miraculous.

Going across to where Philip was, she told him that it had been great to be there, and then asked him the question that had been on her mind for months. It was simply, "How do I go about getting saved?"

Philip was thrilled to hear her ask that question and replied, "Let's talk about that when we get back to Lurgan. We don't need to wait any longer here when you can stop off for as long as you like in our house on your way home."

When they reached their hometown Paul and Steph called into the pastor's home as he had suggested. Jill made tea and toast and all four of them sat around the table in the kitchen, chatting. With the supper over, Philip brought up Steph's earlier enquiry.

"You want to know how to go about getting saved, Steph," he began by way of introduction. "Well let me tell you," and with that he reached for the Bible, which he had kept on the table beside him, and began reading from a number of different places in it. From these Bible references he was able to explain, clearly and simply how to be saved and what it meant to be a Christian.

Steph listened intently to all he had to say and within half-an-hour she had bowed her head and asked God to forgive her sins and Jesus to come into her heart and be her Saviour.

What rejoicing! What an answer to prayer!

Ever since that day back in early January when he had been saved Paul had been praying earnestly that Steph would soon become a Christian too. Now they were united in Christ!

This togetherness was manifest during the week, when Steph found someone to baby-sit with little Ashley and she joined Paul out at the mid-week meeting. It was all so strange to her, but the warmth of the welcome she was given, plus the peace that she had in her heart, made her feel totally at home.

As they were leaving the church that evening Philip said to Paul, "Did your notice that there were no words up on the overhead screens in that meeting on Sunday night?"

"Yes, I did, and I thought it a bit odd," Paul told him. "The screens were in operation at the start, but then when we came to sing they were dead. No words. Nothing."

Philip smiled a funny little mischievous smile before going on, "Well apparently the story is that the man who works the overhead projections in that church is a policeman, and he recognised you when you came in. He must have been afraid you would recognise him and mention him or something for he made himself scarce!"

It was Paul's turn to laugh. "Does he not know that salvation changes a man?" he chuckled. "The old man he once knew is no more. Remember what I shouted the day I was baptised. 'Curly' Winter is dead! He needn't have worried!"

On the next Sunday evening Paul and Steph went out to church together in Emmanuel. Paul felt great. Not only had he been saved but now he also had Steph by his side, in faith and in church.

The church was already packed when they arrived and so the only place Paul and Steph could find a seat was in the very front row. As they were sitting down, Paul was conscious of someone waving across to them. It was Jill. Philip and she were sitting at the other end of the row.

Five minutes later, when the congregation were standing to praise God in wonder and worship Philip came across to where Paul was standing, singing out with all his heart. Placing his hand gently on Paul's shoulder Philip said into his ear, "I had pastor Richard from New Mossley on the phone this afternoon. He was telling me that a young man called Lee came to the Lord during the meeting we were taking there last Sunday night."

More thrilling news! Was there going to be any end to this blessing?

Having delivered that inspirational piece of information Philip moved back across to join Jill and Paul was left feeling ecstatic. He was singing and praising God with such an explosion of energy and spiritual fervour that when the 'worship time' ended he didn't want to sit down. He wasn't ready to sit down! All he wanted to do was go on praising God all evening.

It gave Paul an unbelievable sensation of satisfaction to realise that God had actually used his life to be a witness to Steph, leading eventually to her conversion. Then He had also used his testimony given in a meeting to be at least an influence in seeing a young man come to the Saviour.

Paul felt both humbled and privileged to be used of God like this and it served to fan his already fiercely burning flame of desire to see others brought to faith in Christ.

This passion for personal evangelism surfaced again a few Sundays later when Paul was speaking to a young woman at the end of the morning service. He had seen her at church a number of times previously but as they were walking out beside each other Paul felt moved to enquire, "Are you saved yet, Debbie?"

"No, I'm not. Not yet," the girl replied, bursting into tears.

"Well would you not like to be?" Paul pursued the subject. He had no intention of embarrassing the girl but he was genuinely concerned about her spiritual state, and assumed from her response to his initial enquiry that she was considering salvation seriously.

"Yes, I would," Debbie admitted quietly. It was obvious to Paul that she had been convicted by the direct nature of his approach.

That was all that was said, but as Paul was sitting down to his dinner he felt strongly that he ought to follow up his earlier contact with Debbie by paying her a visit at her home. While eating his meal he kept trying to convince himself that there was no need to rush. He would probably see Debbie out at church again that night, and even if he didn't she would certainly be there the next Sunday morning.

Then there was another consideration. He just remembered that he didn't know her address. Paul had a vague idea of the part of the town she came from, but didn't know exactly where she lived.

Despite these factors, either of which he could have used as an excuse for doing nothing in the meantime, the overriding impulse in Paul's heart was that he had to go that afternoon. Unwilling to stifle such a conviction any longer, Paul said to Steph, "I was speaking to this girl called Debbie in church this morning and I believe she wants to be saved. I'm going round to see her now."

"Where does she live?" Steph asked, quite naturally.

"I'm not really sure," Paul had to confess, "but I know the general area. I will ask somebody and I'm sure I will find her somehow."

It sounded a long shot but Paul was confident that it was the right thing to do and so he slipped a small Bible into his pocket and went out and mounted his bicycle. On reaching the district where he thought the young woman, whom he knew only as Debbie, lived, he enquired of a lady who was walking along the footpath, "Do you know if anybody called Debbie lives around here?"

The woman thought for a moment and then volunteered the information that there was 'a girl' whom she was 'nearly sure was called Debbie,' lived 'somewhere in that next street' but 'she couldn't just be sure of the house.'

"Thank you, that's a good help," Paul told her and cycled on in the direction she had indicated.

When he arrived in the 'next street' he selected a door, as he thought at random, knocked on it and who should open it but Debbie! He had been guided to the exact address!

Trying to disguise his surprise at seeing her at the first door he knocked, Paul greeted Debbie as though he had known precisely where to come. "Hello there," he began cheerily. "Remember we were discussing about you getting saved, at the end of the meeting this morning. I believe God has told me to come round and talk to you more about that. Do you mind if I come in?"

"Not at all, come on," Debbie invited. "I have been thinking about that too."

When they sat down Paul produced his Bible and began to read a selection of relevant verses as Philip had done with him, and he had seen him do with Steph. He used these to tell Debbie about God's provision of salvation and when she said that she understood it and was ready to become a Christian, Paul prayed with her and she trusted Christ.

That night in Emmanuel, with Steph and Debbie both present, Paul was spiritually effervescent, bubbling over with praise to God. He told Philip what had happened with Debbie and his response was, "I knew it was only a matter of time until you led your first soul to the Lord. And I'm sure too that it won't be the last. God is going to use you for His glory."

'For His glory.' The words rang a bell with Paul.

He had heard somebody, a week or two earlier in church, referring to a text in First Peter chapter one, and talking about, 'rejoicing with joy inexpressible and full of glory.'

That was how Paul felt that night!

21

GOD IS SLOWLY CLEANING YOUR SLATE

WHAT PAUL LOVED about being part of Emmanuel Christian Fellowship was that it was more than just a twice-on-a-Sunday-and-once-on-a-weekday church. It was open every day and there was always somebody there to ply with all the questions that kept coming up in his mind as he continued to grow steadily in his faith. He found it comforting to be surrounded by mature and caring Christians. Paul knew that he could always contact Philip, Stephen, Jill or any other member of the church team and be sure of an understanding ear and wise counsel on any subject, at any time.

It was during one of those frequent daytime visits into the church that Philip approached Paul one day. He had the air of someone who had something to say but wasn't just quite sure how best to go about it.

"I wouldn't like you to be offended at this," he began, "but we had the police in here yesterday to warn us about you."

"What do you mean the police were warning you about me?" Paul was a bit bamboozled by this development. "Sure I haven't been in trouble with 'the Peelers' since away back last year."

"I know that," his pastor was quick to reassure him before going on to give more detail about the previous day's encounter. "It was a really high-powered delegation, too. The head of the CID and an Inspector arrived in wanting to know if they could speak to me in confidence. When I brought them into my room they asked me, 'Do you know who it is that you have in here?' I told them that I did and they proceeded to warn me about you."

This both fascinated and frustrated Paul. He thought that after he was saved he would be finished with the police. Now here they were, stalking his footsteps again. He interrupted Philip to ask, "And what exactly were they saying about me?"

"They were saying that Paul Winter had an extensive criminal record and to watch him. If he was coming to church it must be for some ulterior motive. He must see some way of getting something out of it," Philip reported.

Paul couldn't help laughing. "And what did you tell them?" he was keen to know.

"I told them that you had been coming here now for over four months and that we in the church did know about your background. I also told them that we had seen you converted, that we believe that you are a new man, that you have been a blessing to us and that we love you as a Christian," was how the pastor summarised his response.

"Thank you," Paul said, quietly gratified. "If I have been a blessing to you, then you have most definitely been a ten times bigger blessing to me."

Before leaving the subject of Paul and his membership at Emmanuel, Philip reckoned that he might as well tell him the whole story, put him in the picture completely.

"They weren't the first or the only ones, either, mind you, to ask us about you," he informed him. "Every now and again somebody will stop us in the street or a shop and say something like, 'I hear Curly Winter is going to your place. Is that right?'"

"And what do you tell them?" Paul was interested to find out as well. He hadn't been aware that his change of life direction had caused such a stir in Lurgan.

"We say that you do come to us and that we are so pleased to have you here. We tell them that they ought to come to church and meet you and see the change that God has brought about in your life," Philip explained, before going on to add, "Since your baptism we also tell them that the old Curly Winter in dead. They ought to come and meet the new Paul version!"

As he visited the church on various occasions during the day and saw the hive of Christian activity that it represented, Paul longed to become involved in some practical project for God. His public testimony and personal witness had been blessed in seeing others led to Jesus. Now he wanted to help reach out with a helping hand to the local community.

Paul soon found himself praying daily and earnestly, "Lord, please give me something to do for You. I want to reach out to as many people as I can, in Your Name."

One Sunday evening Pastor Mark Hughes was conducting the evening service in Emmanuel and was speaking on the subject of Christian call and commitment. The capacity congregation was challenged by his forthright message and towards the end of it he made an unusual appeal.

"God may be calling you, in this audience, to serve Him in some way, and the one thing he doesn't want to hear from you is your, "Oh no!" he declared.

Leaning forward to the microphone he cupped his hand behind his ear as though intent on listening for or to something, and announced, "What God wants to hear is your 'Oh yes!" Will he hear even one from this large crowd tonight?"

Nobody stirred. There wasn't a sound. A strange hush fell over the congregation.

Leaning ever farther forward, Pastor Hughes cupped his hand even tighter around his ear until it appeared that his fist was almost closed, before repeating his appeal even louder. "God is waiting for an 'Oh yes!' from His people here tonight. Will He hear one, just one...?" he asked.

Paul could not contain his spiritual ardour any longer. Half rising from his seat he called out "Oh yes!" loudly enough for all, including the speaker, to hear.

Pastor Hughes at once pointed down to where Paul was just easing himself back down onto his seat and pronounced, "God bless you brother! God **will** bless you brother!"

During the next week Paul met Iris Loney in Emmanuel one morning. As they were chatting, Iris happened to remark that her husband Andrew was planning to go to Wales the following Monday. On pursuing the subject, Paul discovered that Andrew was taking a van across to collect a load of dolls for the Charity Shop.

"Would there be any chance, do you think, of me going along to give him a hand?" Paul asked her. "I would love to be helping with something like that."

"I don't know," Iris was honest in her answer, "but what I do know is that he always appreciates a bit of company on his trips. Why not ask him? I will give you his mobile number."

When Paul called him up as Iris had suggested, Andrew was glad of the prospect of company and assistance on the run to Wales and the next Monday morning they were on their way.

Since his conversion Paul loved to be in the company of older Christians, hearing them talk about their faith and experiences with God throughout their lives. He found that he invariably learnt something encouraging from them. This could be in the form of a Bible verse which he had never seen before, a couple of lines out of a hymn that he had never heard before, or a series of simple thoughts that lived with him for days.

He found it a blessing to travel with Andrew and talk about a whole range of issues in relation to his Christian faith, and when the two of them were having tea with Wynne, a pastor from Wales, he was given a most valuable, 'Thought for the Day.'

The three men had been busy for the most of the afternoon loading boxes of dolls into the big yellow van, and when they were finished had gone out for a meal together. As they were eating, Paul had been recounting something of his former life and then how he had become a Christian, to Wynne. The pastor was enthralled at his story, and recognising his out-and-out enthusiasm leant forward in his chair and said, "There is something I would like to leave with you, something I believe every young Christian should learn."

Paul leant forward in his chair, anxious not to miss a word of Wynne's wisdom as he went on, "There are three words that you must never forget, for these are the three keywords of Christian service. They are simplicity, obedience and love."

Little did Paul know how soon he was going to be called upon to put this maxim into practice. He would soon find himself having to exercise physical and verbal restraint to a degree which for him would have once been impossible, and Christian love and patience in a very tricky situation.

As they drove towards the harbour in Holyhead, North Wales, to return by ferry to Dublin later that evening Paul noticed that there seemed to be a police car at every roundabout. It crossed his mind at one stage that 'the cops' had their van under surveillance, but then he dismissed the notion as irrelevant. This wasn't a load of guns or detonators they had in the back of the van today. It was a consignment of dolls.

His suspicions were further aroused when they arrived at the port ahead of time. When they asked if they could possibly board an earlier sailing the counter-clerk checked the van's registration on the ticket and told them that it wasn't possible. They would have to wait for the ferry on which they had originally booked. Paul thought this peculiar for at least one man in the queue ahead of them had already had his sailing time brought forward, so there must be space on the boat.

All was to be revealed, however, as they drove forward on the quayside in the line of vehicles waiting to board the ferry. A policeman stepped out in front of them and by a series of gestures indicated to Andrew that he was to pull over and out of the queue.

"Aw no! This doesn't look good, Andrew," Paul predicted. "We are going to get trailed apart here. I feel a bit like Jonah on the boat. This is all because of me. I must be stupid, though, for I just thought that now I'm saved things like this would never happen to me again!"

When they stopped, the policeman asked Andrew to step out of the cab and then directed him into a small room where two other officers were waiting to 'ask him a few questions.' With that duty performed the policeman returned to the van, and climbing up into the back of it began to search through all the boxes of dolls.

As he opened box after box Paul started to walk to and fro in the restricted space in the van beside him, praying that Andrew would soon return and that they would be in time to catch the ferry. He paused in his praying for a minute at one stage. There was something he wanted to know. "I hope you don't mind me asking, but what is your Christian name?" he enquired of the policeman.

"Steve," came the one-word muttered reply.

Paul then raised his hands in the air and continued to pray.

It was now the policeman's turn to be inquisitive. He must have thought he had some kind of a mental case on his hands, for he stopped, knee-deep in plastic dolls, and put his own question.

"If you don't mind me asking, what are you doing?" he wanted to know.

"I'm praying for your salvation," Paul told him without hesitation.

As he was continuing to pray, standing in the back of the van, hands in the air, Paul heard voices coming in his direction. Looking across the parking area he noticed that two policemen were making towards the van. Paul returned to his praying and when he re-opened his eyes they were gone. Perhaps they had decided to leave this queer character to Steve.

It wasn't long after that until Andrew reappeared and told Paul that he was to go in to be questioned. Andrew had told him where to go and when Paul entered the room he found two police officers, a man and a woman, waiting for him.

"Take a seat," the policeman ordered, obviously anxious to get on with the interview.

"No. Hold on a minute," Paul replied. "I'm a Christian now and I want to pray about this. It is important to me to put God first in my life." With that Paul, who remained standing, prayed for Andrew, his work for God, the police officers and their discussion that was about to take place.

Seconds after he had said, 'Amen' the policeman asked, "Well, are you ready to sit down now?"

"Yes, I suppose I am," Paul conceded, and began to give the officers the details they were asking for about the purpose of his trip to Wales. When he had finished, Paul told them how he had been saved and of the joy and peace that he now enjoyed.

"That's all very well," was the policeman's response. "But what about your past? You have quite a colourful criminal record as far as I can make out."

"My past is not a problem," Paul was happy to tell him. "Jesus died on the cross for my past and it has all been forgiven. God doesn't hold it against me any more."

This was a totally new situation for Paul. He had been through dozens of police interrogations in regard to unlawful activity. Now, though, he was being interviewed as a perfectly innocent person, merely trying to assist with charitable Christian work.

Recognising this, Paul continued, "You have had a lot of questions for me and I have answered them all. Now you won't mind if I ask you one. Where will you be when the Lord comes to take the Christians home to heaven?"

The young policewoman laughed. "We'll probably all still be here, partying away as usual!" was her flippant response.

Rising from his chair Paul looked her straight in the eye before giving his reaction to her carefree, contemptuous attitude. "Oh no you won't!" he warned her. "You will be spending a lost eternity in hell."

With that he crossed to the door, opened it and walked out. He then set off down a long corridor towards the door at the other end, which led out into the parking area. He found it strange to walk out unchallenged from a police interview. Although he was always waiting for someone to come running after him, or step out and stop him, it didn't happen.

As Paul was going across to the yellow van, which was now sitting isolated in the park as all the other vehicles had boarded the ferry, he met Steve the policeman on his way back towards the office block.

"Thank you," Steve whispered as their eyes met.

"Thank you," Paul responded. "When I get back home to Northern Ireland I will be telling the people in my church about you and we will be praying for you."

Andrew saw Paul coming and he started the engine of the van. Paul jumped up into his seat in the cab and they were the last vehicle to drive on to the ferry. They had just made it.

When they had settled down to a cup of tea on board they were recounting the day's experiences and Paul was wondering why the police had singled him out yet again.

"There is a perfectly good reason for it," Andrew concluded. "Look at the opportunities you have been given to witness and put the record straight. I believe God is slowly cleaning your slate."

22

WE COULD NEVER AFFORD IT!

SINCE STEPH'S CONVERSION Jill had been coming round to the house every Monday evening to direct her in the basics of Christian living. Steph found this exciting as in each session she discovered more of the joys and privileges of being a child of God. She also found it challenging, though, for one of the first things that Paul and she realised was that now they were joined together in Christ they ought to be joined together in marriage.

They had been living together for years without ever giving it a second thought but when Philip and Jill pointed out to them that marriage had been 'ordained by God' they recognised immediately that they ought to obey God in it. The pastor and his wife counselled and encouraged them and Friday 31 May 2002 was selected as their wedding day.

As they sat discussing the details of 'the big day' Paul began to panic. The ceremony was to be held in Emmanuel Church and they had asked Philip to conduct the service for them. That, for Paul, was the easy bit. Surely that wouldn't cost him anything.

It was when Jill and Steph were going on talking about cars and flowers, a registrar and a reception, and dresses and photographs that he felt the shiver run down his spine. "Hold on there a wee minute," he interrupted at one point, frightened out of his wits. "Where is all the money going to come from to pay for these things you are planning? We are talking about putting on this fancy wedding and we haven't two brown pennies to rub together! Getting married might be the right thing to do O.K., but we could never afford it!"

The trouble was that Paul Winter was no longer living as he once had done. In his former opportunist life style there were always ways and means of doing 'a deal' or 'a job' and making some ready cash, fast. Now, though, he and Steph were happy to readjust to the steal-not defraud-not Christian and legal manner of life. This brought them such joy and peace in their souls, but not so much money in their pockets.

Philip and Jill smiled at one another and then Philip said, "Don't you worry about that. All you have to do is turn up on the day with your guests. We will arrange all the details for you."

This was marvellous. Jill added to Steph's joy by declaring, "You choose a wedding dress and bridesmaids' dresses and we will look after that too. We will put on a good day for you at Emmanuel."

There followed a flurry of activity. They had just a little less than a month to arrange a wedding, but it was done to perfection. That was not to say, though, that on the day there would not be one or two hitches!

The first of these came when Steph was dressing for her big day. She had her dress on and her hair fixed but when she opened the jewel box containing the pearls she had hoped to wear the string was broken and the box contained nothing but a selection of loose pearls of different sizes! Disaster!

She was on the verge of tears and squealed out in anguish, "Oh what am I going to do?" when Jill took over.

There is usually a way out of most minor and momentary crises and Jill Emerson was one of those people who had the uncanny knack of finding it. "Don't cry, Steph," she consoled. "That surely wasn't the only string of pearls in Lurgan. There must be another one somewhere."

With that she beckoned to Stephanie's mum to come with her and the two ladies went out to Jill's car and set off for the nearest jewellers. In fifteen minutes they were back with a replacement string of pearls. Situation saved!

When the bride-to-be was happy that she was ready to venture out on her wedding day the limousine that called to collect her was Kenneth Emerson's Mercedes. It was fitting that Kenneth, who had been instrumental in seeing Paul brought first to church and then to Christ should be the one to bring his bride to his side on their wedding day. Kenneth proved invaluable on the day for he was not only the chauffeur but he also doubled up as photographer for the occasion.

It was a big day out for all the family. Paul's two daughters from his first marriage, Kerri and Leigh, were Steph's bridesmaids and his son Paul was a pageboy. Ashley led her mum up the aisle, strewing rose petals in front of her all the way.

The church had been beautifully decorated for the event. Jill had asked Dorothy, a lady from the fellowship, to do a series of attractive floral arrangements. There were about sixty guests present. The majority of these were from either Paul or Steph's families or from their new Christian family at Emmanuel. Although a few others from Paul's past were invited, only one came. He had been to Emmanuel with Paul the first night he had attended, under the influence of drink. Now he had come to see him married in the church. Wee Rab.

As Philip was conducting the ceremony and Paul and Steph were about to take their vows, standing in front of him, the bride began to feel dizzy. She looked across at Paul and whispered,

"I'm going to collapse!" Philip heard Steph's muted message and noticed the colour drain from her cheeks. He was about to signal for somebody to bring forward a chair when a lady guest saw what was happening and placed one behind the swaying bride.

Stephanie is taller than Paul so after she was seated and her husband-to-be had checked that she was well enough, he observed aloud, "It's just as well you had to sit down. At least I won't have to get somebody to lift me up so that I can kiss you now!"

When it came time for Paul to affirm that he 'took this woman to be his lawful wedded wife' he could barely wait. Philip hadn't even finished the question before he looked down at Steph beside him and declared his resounding, "I do!"

It was that kind of service all the way through, happy and relaxed. All Paul and Steph wanted to do was obey God in marriage and they were most anxious that all their friends and relatives should enjoy the experience along with them.

After Mr. and Mrs. Winter had signed the register at the front of the church many of their guests crowded around to congratulate the newly weds. When they managed to tear themselves away from the different groups of well-wishers Paul and Steph set off in chauffeur-driven style for Tannaghmore Gardens, a few miles out of town.

Kenneth, their driver, friend and photographer had brought them there as it was an ideal setting in which to take a few photographs to record the day for posterity. Little did Paul and Steph know, however, but the photographer had been encouraged to take as long as he liked over the photos because 'the caterers' needed some time. While all the different combinations of close family were being captured on film Emmanuel Church in Union Street had been turned into a veritable hive of activity.

When all those who had been out at the photographic session returned to the church they found it transformed. A group of ladies had been very busy preparing food and Paul, Stephanie and their families returned to find a buffet meal ready for everyone. The church leaders had assured the couple that they would give them and all their guests 'a good day' and they had certainly kept their promise.

Paul and Stephanie were overwhelmed. Later in the evening, after everyone had eaten, Paul, in the course of a speech in which he was constantly thanking everybody for their kindness, made it clear why he had, at first, found all this Christian love and generosity hard to fathom. "You see, in the life I once lived, in the world where I once operated, nobody gave you anything for nothing," he explained. "If somebody did you a favour they expected something from you in return, and if you didn't live up to expectations things could turn nasty."

"It's not like that here," he went on. "From the very day I got saved everybody in this place has been so good to me, and then when Steph became a Christian it was the same for her too. It used to be that I could never figure this out, but I can now. I have discovered that our friends in Emmanuel are so loving and generous because they recognise that God has been loving and generous to them. Their kindness is merely a practical expression of the love of God in their hearts.

There is a verse in the Bible that says, 'My God shall supply all your need according to His riches in glory by Christ Jesus.' When we were talking about getting married a month or so ago I remember telling somebody that marriage might be the right thing to do but we could never afford it!

We needn't have worried. Our God has supplied all our need, using these wonderful servants of His around me here. We just want to praise Him for everything!"

23

WHAT'S GOING ON HERE, GOD?

IN THE LATE summer of 2002 Paul began to feel unwell. He had just got a job but was finding regular work difficult. This was not that the work was hard, but because he never felt up to it for he was constantly under par.

When he complained to Steph, saying, "I don't feel very well," she would tell him to remember the life he had once lived. Although she had an occasional niggling suspicion that perhaps there was actually something wrong with her husband she tried to play down his moping and moaning.

"Think of where you've come from," she would protest, trying to console herself as well as Paul, "You nearly wrecked your body with drink and drugs. Is it any wonder you don't feel very well every now and again?"

The lethargy and sickness persisted on into the autumn and it was then that Paul asked the elders to pray with him. They agreed to do this and they also encouraged him to go and see a doctor.

As he was leaving the room after the prayer session, Stephen remarked to Philip, "Paul is not well. I know by the look of him. We must continue to pray that he will be all right."

When Paul made an appointment with the doctor he arranged for him to have a number of X-rays. The results of these, when they came back, caused Paul some alarm and the doctor set up an urgent hospital appointment for him.

"The X-rays are showing a tumour on a testicle," he explained to the shocked patient, "and I would like you to see a consultant over at Craigavon Hospital as soon as possible."

A tumour. The word had a sinister sound. Paul found it menacing, somehow. What was happening to him?

His hospital appointment was made for a Friday and the consultant examined Paul, and his records and X-rays, before coming up with his diagnosis. "There would seem to be no doubt that you have testicular cancer," he stated very simply. "I will make arrangements for you to be admitted on Sunday afternoon for surgery on Monday. By this time next week it will be away and you should be starting to feel better."

Paul drove home from hospital in a daze. He could hardly take it in.

The word 'tumour' a week or so ago had set the alarm bells ringing in his mind.

The word 'cancer' that day had sparked a full-scale alert.

While grappling to come to terms with this news he kept half-praying half-questioning. "What is going on here, God?" he would enquire, desperately. "I'm saved, and I thank You for that and for all that You've given me and done for me. But why have I got cancer? Why are You allowing this to happen to me?"

Having first gone home to tell Steph the news Paul then went on to Emmanuel. He had long since discovered that it was always good to meet with the sympathetic believers down there in times of doubt and difficulty.

When he had spoken to a number of his friends in the fellowship and they had prayed with him Paul was standing chatting to Stephen, the assistant pastor, before leaving for home.

They were discussing the seriousness and incidence of testicular cancer when Stephen remarked, "Yes. I know a number of men who have had it. In fact one of the last ones was my brother-in-law."

"Oh is that right?" Paul replied. "And how is he now?"

Stephen hesitated a moment before replying, "It was very sad. He didn't make it. He died."

Although Stephen went on to say that he knew dozens of men who had gone for the operation and were 'living normal lives,' the prospect of death as an ultimate outcome of his condition had a sobering effect on Paul. When he went into hospital on Sunday afternoon it was with a strange mixture of concern and confidence.

The confidence came from the knowledge that he had committed his life into the hands of God, whatever happened, and that hundreds of people from the town and district had promised to pray for him.

The concern stemmed from a natural trepidation about the future. What would happen if the operation were not a success? He couldn't help thinking about Stephen's brother in law now and again. He 'hadn't made it.' In his 'down' moments there was always the irritating query, to which there didn't seem to be an obvious answer, 'Why me?'

When he was shown into the ward which was to be his base for the next few days he found that God had somebody there who would help him out of his present self-pity and the dread of the operation that was scheduled for the next day.

The lad in the bed beside him was paraplegic. He could do absolutely nothing for himself. As Paul saw the nursing staff work with him, he reflected on the fact that he had all his faculties, and on top of that he had God. Before his surgery the next afternoon Paul had begun to thank God humbly for the promise of His presence and the prayers of His people.

Such had his preoccupation with the Lord become that he woke up in the recovery room after the operation with his hands in the air. He was singing in a dry, cracked voice, "All for Jesus! All for Jesus!"

Later that evening, back in the ward, Paul wanted to read his Bible. It had been an anxious day, and now he felt he needed to spend time in the presence of God. There was a constant buzz of activity around the ward and he found it impossible to concentrate so clutching his Bible and book of Daily Readings he set off for the Quiet Room.

It wasn't easy. There were times that he felt so dizzy that he was sure he must have been bouncing off the walls. He made it though, and when he sat down he had to rest for a while to allow the nausea, brought on by the effort, to settle.

Concentrating was a problem, but still Paul was determined to read his Bible. He felt that God had a message of comfort and encouragement for him from His Word. And He had.

The selected reading for the day from his notes was Isaiah chapter 12, and when Paul turned to it he was thrilled to read the second verse. It said, 'Behold God is my salvation, I will trust, and not be afraid; The Lord, Jehovah, is my strength and song; He also is become my salvation.'

What assurance! God was his strength, his song and his salvation. What was there to fear? Surely he could 'trust and not be afraid.'

Paul struggled back to his bed with a much lighter heart. Although he was still suffering from the after-effects of the anaesthetic, the operation was over and it had been a success. God was in charge.

The following afternoon Paul was sitting up in bed reading a book that someone had recommended he 'take in with him.' It was, they said, 'about a guy called Thomas Martin and he had a background very much like your own. You would enjoy it.'

The book was called 'Out of The Maze,' and Paul was enjoying it as had been predicted. He had just set it down upside down and open at his place when a nurse came along on her rounds.

She glanced at the cover, and fascinated by the title, 'Out of the Maze,' she went on to read the subtitles, 'Aggressive Teenager and Paramilitary Prisoner. The tremendous story of the transformation in the life of Thomas Martin.' Her curiosity must have been sufficiently aroused for she then picked up the book, and turning it over to where Paul had been reading she began to read a paragraph or two herself.

A few moments later the nurse returned the book to the position on the bed from which she had lifted it, with the comment, "That's very deep, rough stuff. Could you not have picked a book with a happier ending?"

Paul had been watching in silence while she read, and had been wondering what she was thinking. Now that he knew he had the answer to her observation.

"An ex-paramilitary man finds salvation. A girl comes to visit him in prison and they get married, have a family and are living happily ever after. He has also even become the minister of a church. Surely you couldn't dream up any happier ending than that. They don't come any happier than that!"

After being discharged from hospital Paul made steady progress both physically and spiritually. God blessed Steph and he with Billie-Jo, a little sister for Ashley, and as a family they continued to rejoice in the bountiful provision of the Lord.

Paul was also happy to become involved in as much work as he could in Emmanuel and when he learnt that Alan Emerson from the church was hoping to organise a mission trip to Africa he was keen to find out all the details. On discovering that the trip, which was organised in conjunction with the Christian charity Habitat for Humanity, was to Uganda, and was departing on 3 July 2004, he was one of the first to volunteer.

There were 16 in the group that went out from Lurgan and for Paul, and all the others who were making their first trip to Africa, Uganda was a terrible culture shock. They found what they would describe as 'the absolute poverty of the people,' distressing.

Coming from a country where the prayer of many of the Christian people was, 'Lord help me to lose a pound or two this week,' to a land where the Christians were praying, 'Lord just give me enough to feed my family today,' was an eye-opener.

Coming from a country where people had so many clothes that they could barely close their wardrobe doors to a land where men and boys had often just one shirt and it possibly in holes, and women and girls had one frock each, and it possibly patched, was a revelation.

Paul had a heart for the children and before leaving home he had bought a huge consignment of sweets and he gave one to every child he met, for as long as they lasted. This led to him being accorded the nickname of the words in the local language meaning, 'lover of children.'

Uganda had been a tremendous spiritual experience for Paul but about two weeks after he returned to Northern Ireland he took what he thought was the flu. He had a very high temperature, constant sore heads and he could never seem to be able to keep himself warm. Although it was summer, and pleasant weather, Paul had the central heating on in the house to try and keep some heat in his body.

The symptoms were particularly bad and Paul felt thoroughly miserable one evening when a friend rang up to enquire how he was. On hearing him describe his condition she advised him to contact a doctor as soon as possible. "Remember where you have been Paul Winter," she cautioned. "It could be more than just the flu you have."

Conceding that perhaps she 'could have a point,' Paul phoned the out of hours doctor and was invited to 'come down to the clinic.' Before leaving for the appointment Paul filled his pockets with tracts, somehow strangely conscious that he probably wouldn't be back home for a while. Whatever it was that was wrong with him might take more than a prescription and bottle of pills to treat.

When the 'out of hours' doctor had examined Paul he said, "I want you to go around to the Accident and Emergency Unit in the hospital as soon as you leave me here. I will tell them you are coming."

It didn't sound good, but Paul didn't feel good, and so he was glad to be going across to A & E. The staff there examined him thoroughly and took some blood samples and then escorted him around to a side ward with only one bed in it.

Paul was surprised to find a young lady doctor there to meet him. "Good evening Mr. Winter, we have been waiting for you," was her friendly greeting. "I will be along to get some details from you in five or ten minutes, after you have settled into bed."

True to her word she reappeared about ten minutes later, clipboard in hand. She asked Paul about his medical history, ticking boxes and making notes on a series of pages on her board.

As she was coming near the end of it Paul felt free to ask her the question that was on his mind, "What do you think is wrong with me?"

"Your symptoms would appear to indicate that you have malaria," she informed him. "I'm quite sure that this will be confirmed when all our test results come back."

Malaria! So that's why the friend on the phone had told him to remember where he had been.

Having completed her medical questionnaire the young doctor slipped her pen into the top of the clipboard, which she then placed on the edge of the locker. Then leaning forward in her chair she looked Paul in the eye and enquired, "Are you a Christian?"

"Yes. I am," Paul told her, pleasantly surprised. "How did you know?"

"So am I," the girl replied with a smile. "I have heard about you."

Paul had always loved to meet Christians. No matter where he came across them he found that he was drawn to them with an instant bond of brotherhood. It was no different that day. This young doctor was his sister in Christ.

The pair in the ward, doctor and patient, began a brief interchange about when they had become Christians and what churches they attended, before the doctor asked Paul another question.

No wonder she had set her clipboard over to the one side. This question wasn't on any of her sheets.

"Do you mind if I pray with you?" she enquired.

"Not at all," Paul replied. To have a Christian doctor pray with him sounded like a good way to start his stay in hospital.

The doctor then sat on the edge of the bed, took Paul's hand and began to pray with him. As she prayed for healing in the name of the Lord Jesus the patient came to realise just how ill he was and also what it meant to have faith in One who, in the Bible, healed all kinds of diseases. It was scary when she prayed through all the medical complications that could occur with malaria, but comforting when the young doctor went on to pray for complete and absolute healing from the disease.

Paul thanked her profusely for her professional skill and her heartfelt prayer before she left to go on about her duties. He felt that this stay in hospital had commenced on a very spiritual note, with God having assigned one of His children to welcome him in, and it could probably be used for His glory.

It was too. It wasn't long until Paul had exhausted the supply of tracts he had brought in with him and had to ask Steph to bring him more. Lots of Christians from the various evangelical churches in the town called to visit him and pray for his recovery.

Although Paul was always delighted to see them and appreciated their concern for him, he never missed an opportunity to speak to any non-Christian, entering the ward, about his faith.

Anyone, whether a member of the hospital staff or a visitor who enquired, as a part of polite conversation, "What were you doing out in Africa?" was given a two fold answer. The opening part of it told of a Christian mission to Uganda, and this was inevitably followed up by how he had become a Christian in the first place. Those who showed any interest were offered, and usually took, a gospel tract from him.

Paul was in hospital for six days and on his fifth morning one of the nurses came to him and said, "See you. After listening to you all me and my husband talked about last night was God." It was passed off as a joke but Paul could see that underneath she had been quite affected by his witness.

"That's great!" Paul replied, delighted. "I will just be praying that soon you and your husband will not only talk about God, but will come to know Him in a personal way. I believe that's why God has put me in here for a while, just to meet people like you."

It was only sometime later, when Paul was reflecting on what he had said to that nurse that it dawned on him that he had actually answered his own question, asked in anguish about a previous hospital visit.

It was, "What's going on here, God?"

24

I KNOW WHO YOU ARE NOW!

THE YOUNG DOCTOR'S prayers were answered. Paul made a complete recovery and life for him came gradually back to normal. He had obtained full time employment and was thus assured of a steady income with which to support his wife and growing family.

The main focus of his life, though, was trying to see others reached for Jesus. Coming to know the Saviour had made such a profound difference to every aspect of life for Paul that he wanted everybody else to experience the peace and satisfaction that he was enjoying daily.

He found that one of the most rewarding ways in which he could witness to others about his faith in Christ was to join the outreach team from Emmanuel Church working on the streets of Lurgan every Friday night. This group met in the church for prayer and then dispersed to different locations around the town where young people would be liable to congregate. As they met them outside the various entertainment centres Paul and his friends would then help them and talk to them as the opportunity presented itself.

One Friday night in November 2005 Paul was out on the streets with this group and was chatting to a gang of young lads who had a few drinks taken. They stood around asking questions about why a number of people should be out on the town showing any kind of interest in them.

As they talked Paul was aware that one of the chaps, who was having difficulty standing without staggering, and so had plonked himself with his back against a wall, was staring intently at him. "I recognise you from somewhere," he kept saying, leaning forward and clicking his fingers as though to stir his befuddled memory into action. "I'm sure I have seen you before..."

Paul just smiled. He thought he knew the lad, but had no desire to attempt to recall the context in which they had previously met. It was one of many episodes from the past that was much better forgotten.

The conversation continued amongst the crowd on the footpath until another lad in his late teens came along. He was also a bit tipsy, but he had no difficulty recognising one of the former hard men of the town.

Walking right up to Paul he gave him a solid thump, shoulder to shoulder, shouting as he did so, "How are you Curly? Long time no see!"

This greeting acted as the spark that fired the memory of the finger-clicking fellow against the wall. "I know who you are now! You're Curly Winter!" he exclaimed. "That's it! You were involved in the paramilitaries. You were up to your neck in them! I knew I had seen you before!"

Paul was moving across to speak to him on his own, but before he could get a chance to say a word the former associate was going on, "You have given up an awful lot to be out here!"

"Don't worry, mate! I haven't given up anything!" Paul was quick to reassure him. "I have gained everything!"

This afforded Paul an ideal opportunity to tell the lad what God had done for him, and the fulfilled life he was now leading, and he took it. When he had finished a short but pithy summary of his personal testimony Paul encouraged the lad and his friends to go down to the youth meeting going on at that time in Emmanuel Church.

Somewhat to Paul's surprise a few of them agreed to go. They possibly felt a bit new and strange, or maybe they weren't either quite clear enough in their minds or steady enough on their feet, but they didn't take part in anything that was going on around them. They merely sat in a corner whispering amongst themselves, with the leaders stopping occasionally to have a chat with them.

Before the boys left that Friday night they were invited back to the Sunday evening service but those who bothered to respond at all replied with a rather non-committal, "Aye, I might." The young man who had tried so hard to recognise Paul on the Friday night did go, however, and at the end of the service surrendered his life to the Lord.

When Paul's dad passed away his mum came to live with Steph and he in Lurgan. She settled in very well to her new home in the County Armagh town and loved having such close contact with her grandchildren. There were now three of them for her son and daughter-in-law had become the proud parents of a third daughter, Rachel.

One of the few features of her former life in Dundonald that she missed was her attendance at Ballybeen Mission Hall and the Christian fellowship of the women there, many of whom she had known since childhood. Paul had always told her, "Don't worry, mum, some Sunday night when I'm free I'll take you back to Ballybeen."

The problem was that Paul was so involved with his activities in Emmanuel that it was early in 2006 before he was in a position to keep his promise.

From the moment he had arranged with his mum to take her back to her roots in Ballybeen until the moment they set out for Dundonald, Paul was startled to find himself engaged in a mental battle with his past.

"What are you going back there for?" he kept thinking.

" Do you not remember what you were like when you lived there?" something kept reminding him. "You were so bad that they threw you out of that Sunday School for being constantly disruptive."

Paul overcame those thoughts, recognising that they were from the Devil. Satan did not want him going back to his old haunts in the power of the Spirit of God. When he began to remind himself that it was not the former, uncontrollable Curly Winter but a new creation in Christ Jesus that was returning to Ballybeen, he set off happily with his mum.

It had been well over a year since June, his mother, had been back in the Mission Hall there and in the car on the way up from Lurgan to Belfast she found it difficult to disguise her excitement. She had always wanted to pay her old friends a visit and now she was going back. Some of the people she mentioned Paul knew and others he didn't, but it made no difference. Mum kept rattling on about them until Paul and she arrived at their destination.

Heads began to turn when Paul and his mum walked slowly up the aisle in the middle of Ballybeen Mission Hall, looking to find a suitable seat. They hadn't been sitting for anything more than seconds until virtually everyone in the building knew they were there, and who they were. A nudge with the elbow followed by a deliberate directional point with the head accompanied by a loud whisper, for many of the congregation were growing old and had already gone deaf, announced the return of the prodigal.

"It's Paul. Do you not remember Paul Winter? That's him over there with June, his mother. She used to come here every week until her husband died and then she went to live with Paul and the wife away in Lurgan or somewhere," was a typical message on the Ballybeen bush telegraph.

The service was about to begin and as the congregation sang the first hymn Paul felt a warm glow inside. He was glad that he had offered to bring his mum back to Ballybeen for this was a touching homecoming for him. Once, as a boy he had been an absolute pest in this place, but now he had returned as a member of the family.

Ernie Shooter from the Belfast City Mission, who was the man in charge of the outreach in Ballybeen was already on the platform when Paul arrived into the Hall, and when he saw him in the audience he welcomed him with a nod of recognition and a broad smile. Paul was not quite prepared, though, for what he was going to say when making his announcements and outlining the order of service.

"We are delighted to have Paul Winter back with us in Ballybeen," Ernie told the congregation, "and after we have sung this next hymn he will be coming up here to give us a word of testimony."

Paul didn't have much time to prepare, but he didn't need much time to prepare. The very fact that he was there at all was a tremendous witness in itself. Everybody just wanted to see him on the platform and when he began to tell them about his early life there were occasional interjections.

As he was describing some of his earlier escapades an elderly man muttered loudly enough for everyone to hear, "Aye, you're right. You were a real bad 'un!"

When Paul came to tell of the morning just over four years before when he trusted Christ, the audience made no effort to restrain a spontaneous chorus of 'Amen' and 'Praise the Lord!'

While the local lad was returning to his seat, after having given God the glory for all He had done in his life, Ernie Shooter added a few of his own recollections of what Paul had been like to work with in his earlier days. Before concluding his remarks he looked down and said, "Thank you, Paul. You may not even realise it, but there were buckets of tears shed for you in this very Hall in the prayer meetings. You are a real trophy of God's grace!"

Nobody was in any hurry away at the close of the service. Most of those present wanted to speak to their visiting friends from Lurgan, so much so that Paul was overwhelmed.

He could hardly believe it. These sincere Christian people had been praying for him all down the years. Now there he was, back as a transformed person, a tangible answer to all those passionate prayers.

Ernie was waiting for him in the porch.

Gripping Paul firmly by the hand, he said, "Maybe you'll come back again some time, Paul, and take another meeting for us."

"Maybe I will, Ernie," Paul replied. "But when I come the next time I will let you know well in advance so that you can announce that I will be here. It's not that I want people to come to see me, or anything like that. All I want is for them to see what 'a trophy of God's grace' as you call me, looks like!"

"Don't worry," Ernie assured him. "You'll be back. Everybody round here knows what you were like years ago. I would just love to give them the chance to look at you and listen to you. Let them find out who you are now!"

Other books by the same author

———•—•———

MY FATHER'S HAND
THIS IS FOR REAL
JUST THE WAY I AM
SOME PARTY IN HEAVEN
FIRST CITIZEN SMYTH
SOMETHING WORTH LIVING FOR
HOW SWEET THE SOUND
AS OUR HEADS ARE BOWED
ONLY THE BEST WILL DO
A BRUISED REED
BACK FROM THE BRINK
OUT OF THE MAZE
THE TANGLED LAMB
SOLDIER, SAILOR, LIVE OR DIE
I BELIEVE GOD
PAINTING THE TOWN RED
WHO CARES?
SIGN OF THE FISH
OUT OF THE DEEP
NOT BY MIGHT
A LITTLE CHILD SHALL LEAD THEM
AS WHITE AS SNOW

———•—•———

Contact Ambassador Productions +44 (0) 28 9045 0010
for your nearest stockist

www.ambassador-productions.com